THE ROANOKE COLONY

AMERICA'S FIRST MYSTERY

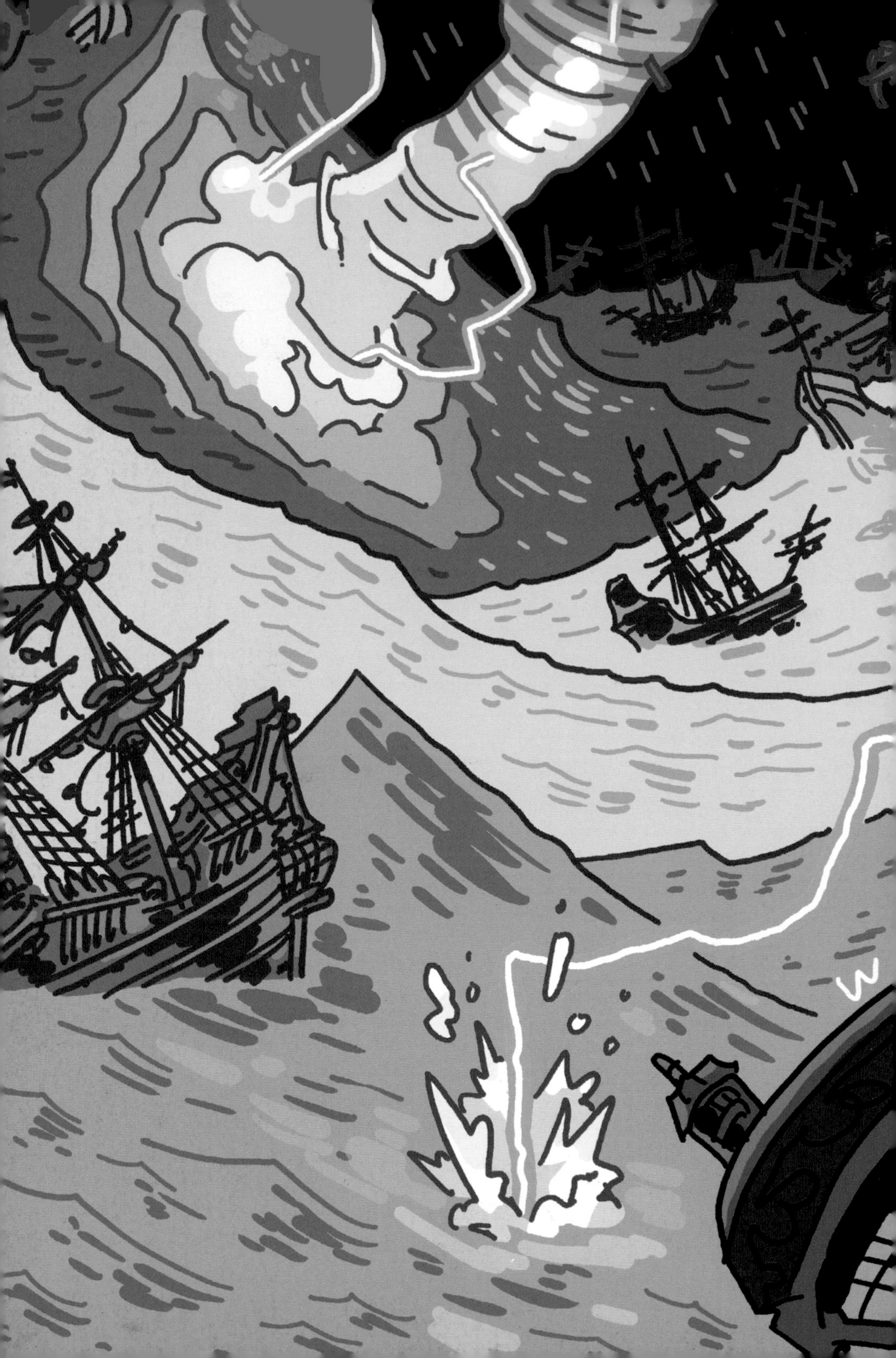

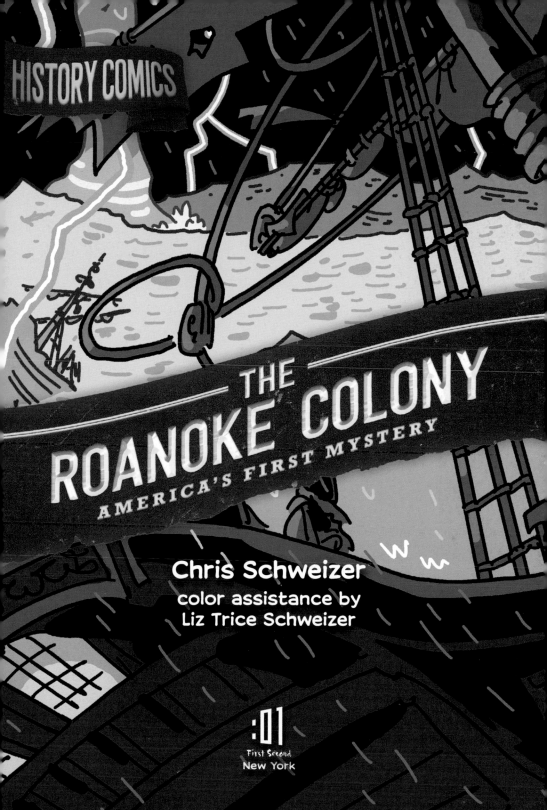

HISTORY COMICS

THE ROANOKE COLONY
AMERICA'S FIRST MYSTERY

Chris Schweizer
color assistance by
Liz Trice Schweizer

:01
First Second
New York

First Second

Copyright © 2020 by Chris Schweizer

Published by First Second
First Second is an imprint of Roaring Brook Press, a division of Holtzbrinck Publishing
Holdings Limited Partnership
120 Broadway, New York, NY 10271

Don't miss your next favorite book from First Second! For the latest updates go to
firstsecondnewsletter.com and sign up for our enewsletter.

Library of Congress Control Number: 2019938067

Paperback ISBN: 978-1-250-17435-2
Hardback ISBN: 978-1-250-17434-5

Our books may be purchased in bulk for promotional, educational, or business use. Please
contact your local bookseller or the Macmillan Corporate and Premium Sales Department
at (800) 221-7945 ext. 5442 or by email at MacmillanSpecialMarkets@macmillan.com.

First edition, 2020
Edited by Dave Roman
Cover design by Kirk Benshoff
Interior book design by Angela Boyle
Consultant on Algonquin culture: Evan T. Pritchard
Color assistance by Liz Trice Schweizer

Penciled, inked, and colored digitally in Adobe Photoshop with the pencil and paint
bucket tool.

Printed in China by Toppan Leefung Printing Ltd., Dongguan City, Guangdong Province
Paperback: 10 9 8 7 6 5 4 3 2 1
Hardcover: 10 9 8 7 6 5 4 3 2 1

When I was a kid, I had a book called (something like) *Teenage Historical Stories* that told true stories of kids who played important roles in well-known events in history. I can't find it online, so maybe I have the title wrong, but I remember the book vividly and the great impact it had on me. Partly because of the books I read and partly because I grew up in North Dakota, where the feeling of the frontier was still very much alive, I have always liked history.

When I became a professional historian, I decided to make the earliest period of transatlantic contacts and colonization my specialty. I like this period because, especially in the case of English venturers, none of them actually knew what they were doing. They were all making it up as they went along, and hoping that some of their tactics might actually work, like throwing spaghetti at the wall and seeing if any stuck.

Atlantic ventures favored brave and clever people, and kids were the most successful at reinventing themselves in new situations. Everyone knew that kids were less threatening than adults and would be welcomed into alien communities, and that they could adapt to new and different lifestyles and could learn languages much better than grown-ups. Leaders on both sides in America sent boys to live with the other side in hopes that they would become go-betweens and translators with good access in the future.

The Roanoke colonies offer many examples of young people stepping up and taking center stage. Manteo and Wanchese were probably still in their teens when they volunteered to go to London in 1584. Their goal was to learn more about the newcomers so they could manage relationships when the English returned. Many European ships had traveled along the coast by this time, so the Roanokes already knew a lot more about people from across the ocean than the English knew about them. And Manteo and Wanchese were not the first. A boy named Paquiquineo had boarded a Spanish ship that came to the Carolina coast in 1561, and he lived with the Spanish in the Caribbean, Mexico, and Spain for a full decade. A fifteen-year-old French boy, Guillaume Rouffin, was left behind by a French colony on the Carolina coast when colonists departed in a hurry a few years later. He lived with Guale Indians for two years before Spanish colonists took him to live with them in Florida, where he became the interpreter known as Guillermo Rufin.

We don't know what happened to the Lost Colonists, but if they followed all the others who had been left behind and

became American Natives, the adjustment must have been weird. For one thing, English clothes were very complicated and came in parts that had to be laced or buckled together. The clothes they now wore were really simple and exposed a lot of skin. Instead of hard-soled shoes, they wore moccasins. Kids would have adapted a lot easier than adults, and they may have liked the freedom of such loose clothing. Their new houses and food would not have been very different from what they were used to, except that they would have had a lot more fruits and vegetables. Sleeping all together in a longhouse was absolutely normal. No one in England had a single room or even a single bed, except maybe Queen Elizabeth and even she was never completely alone. Boys and men would have had to learn to use a bow and arrows, and how to fish and hunt, and girls and women would have worked to grow the crops and prepare food alongside Native women of all ages. They had to adapt in order to survive. No English pomposity allowed.

If they did join the Roanokes or other tribes, how much time went by before the former colonists stopped thinking of themselves as English and began to fit in so much that they identified with the people they now lived with? If Jamestown colonists who arrived twenty years later actually looked some of the Roanoke colonists in the face would they have recognized them as English? Soon after the newcomers arrived in 1607, George Percy saw "a Savage Boy about the age of ten years, which had a head of hair of a perfect yellow and a reasonable white skin." Percy did not say anything more about the boy, but the English must have wondered about him. Unfortunately they had just arrived and did not have anyone who could understand his language. Although a small group went down to the Carolina coast to see what they could find, the Jamestown colonists learned nothing about the Roanoke lost colonists. Henry Fleet, a Jamestown colonist who lived with Anacostia Indians for five years after being captured said he spoke the Anacostians' language much better than "mine own." What would all the various Lost Colonists have remembered after twenty years?

—**Karen Ordahl Kupperman,**
Author of *Roanoke: The Abandoned Colony*

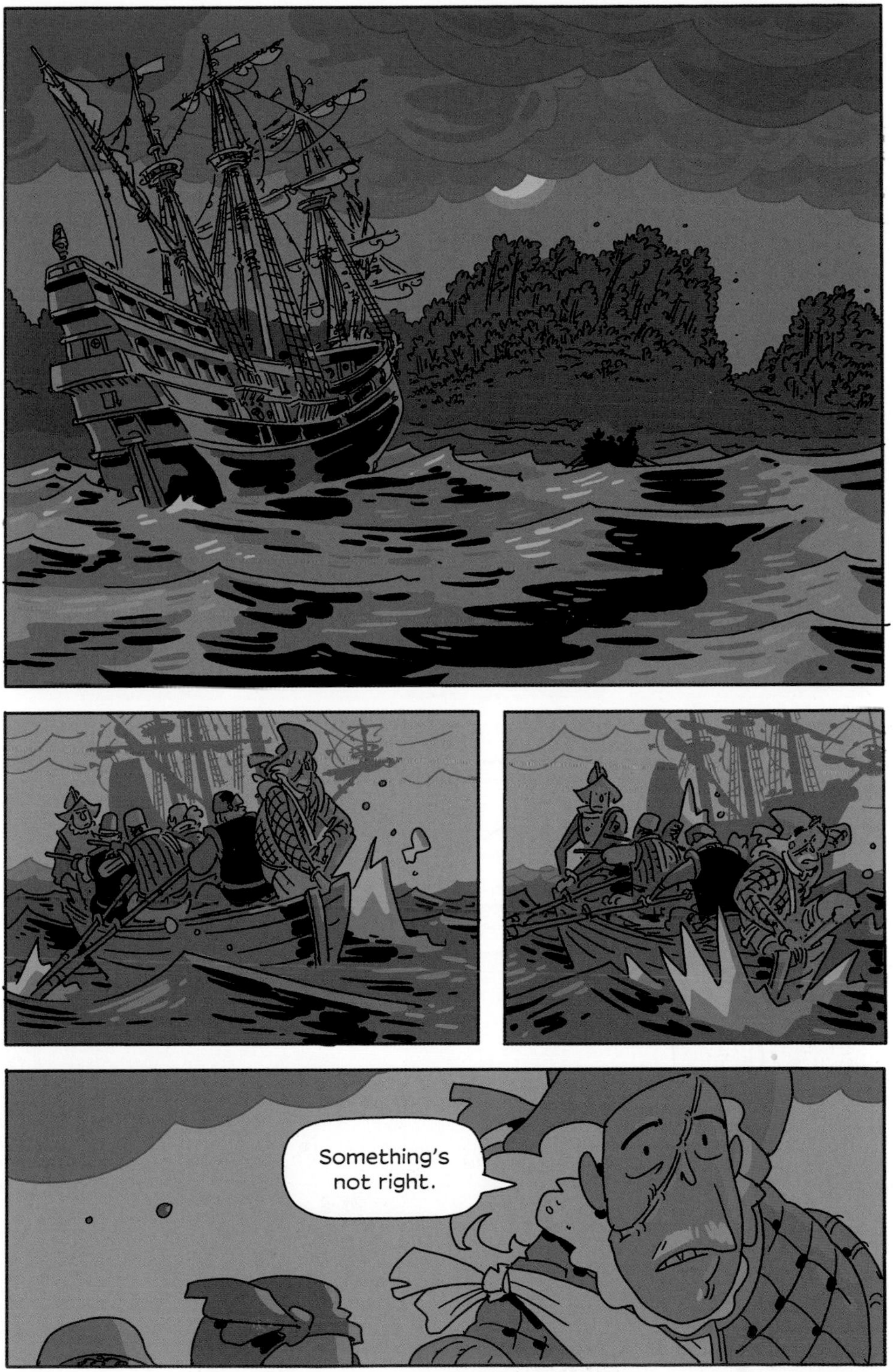
Something's
not right.

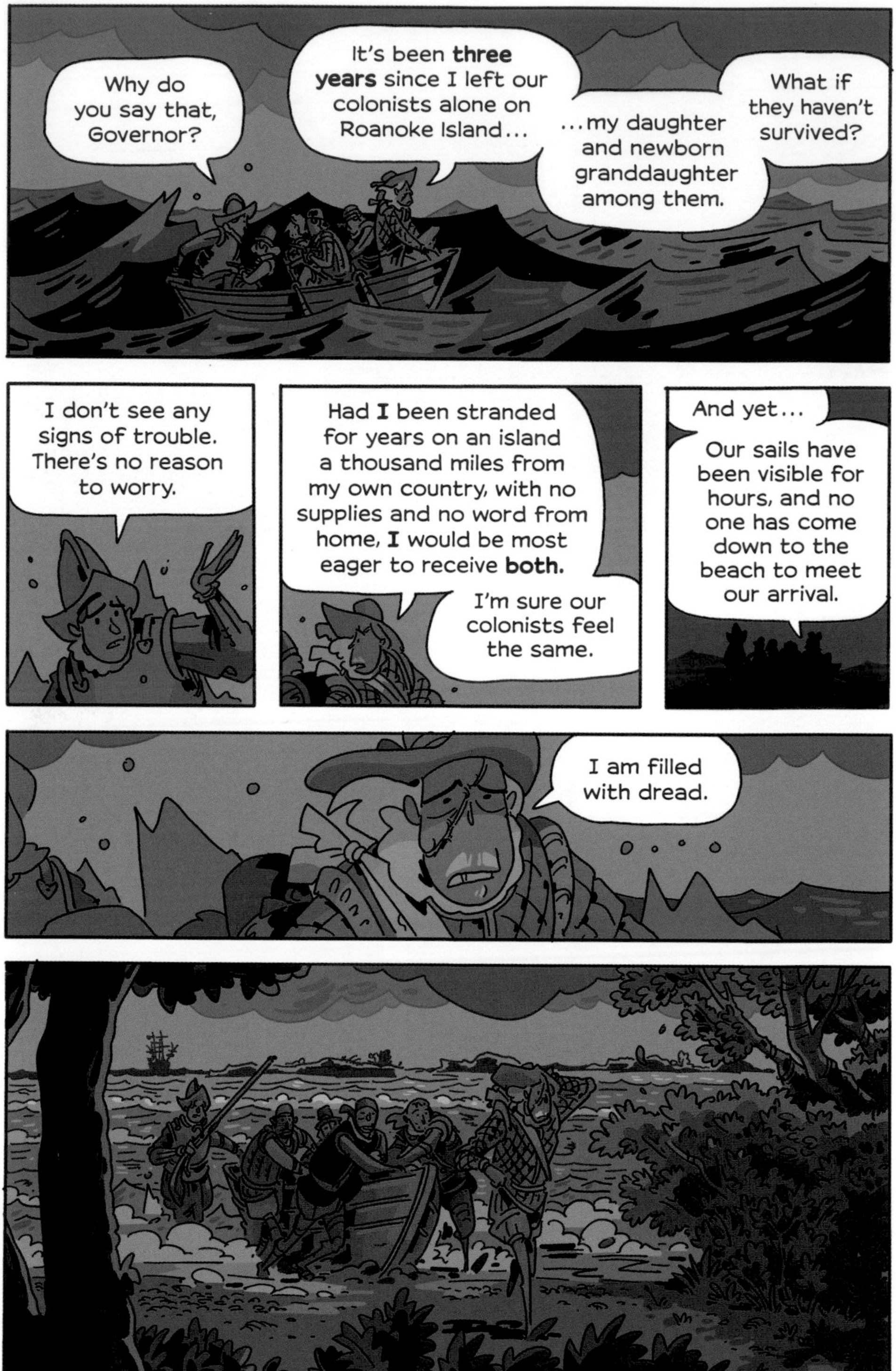
Why do you say that, Governor?
It's been **three years** since I left our colonists alone on Roanoke Island...
...my daughter and newborn granddaughter among them.
What if they haven't survived?
I don't see any signs of trouble. There's no reason to worry.
Had **I** been stranded for years on an island a thousand miles from my own country, with no supplies and no word from home, **I** would be most eager to receive **both.**
I'm sure our colonists feel the same.
And yet...
Our sails have been visible for hours, and no one has come down to the beach to meet our arrival.
I am filled with dread.

Good heavens!

That fence...

...that **palisade**...

...it wasn't here before.

If all of the buildings are now **inside** that palisade, that at least explains why no one has yet seen us.

Still...
I worry.

The only reason they would have built that fence is for **protection**.

What were they protecting themselves **against**?

Hello!

Hello, the town!

Why does no one answer?

There **is** a storm coming. Maybe they're all inside the houses.

Hello!

Governor White! I've found the gate leading inside.

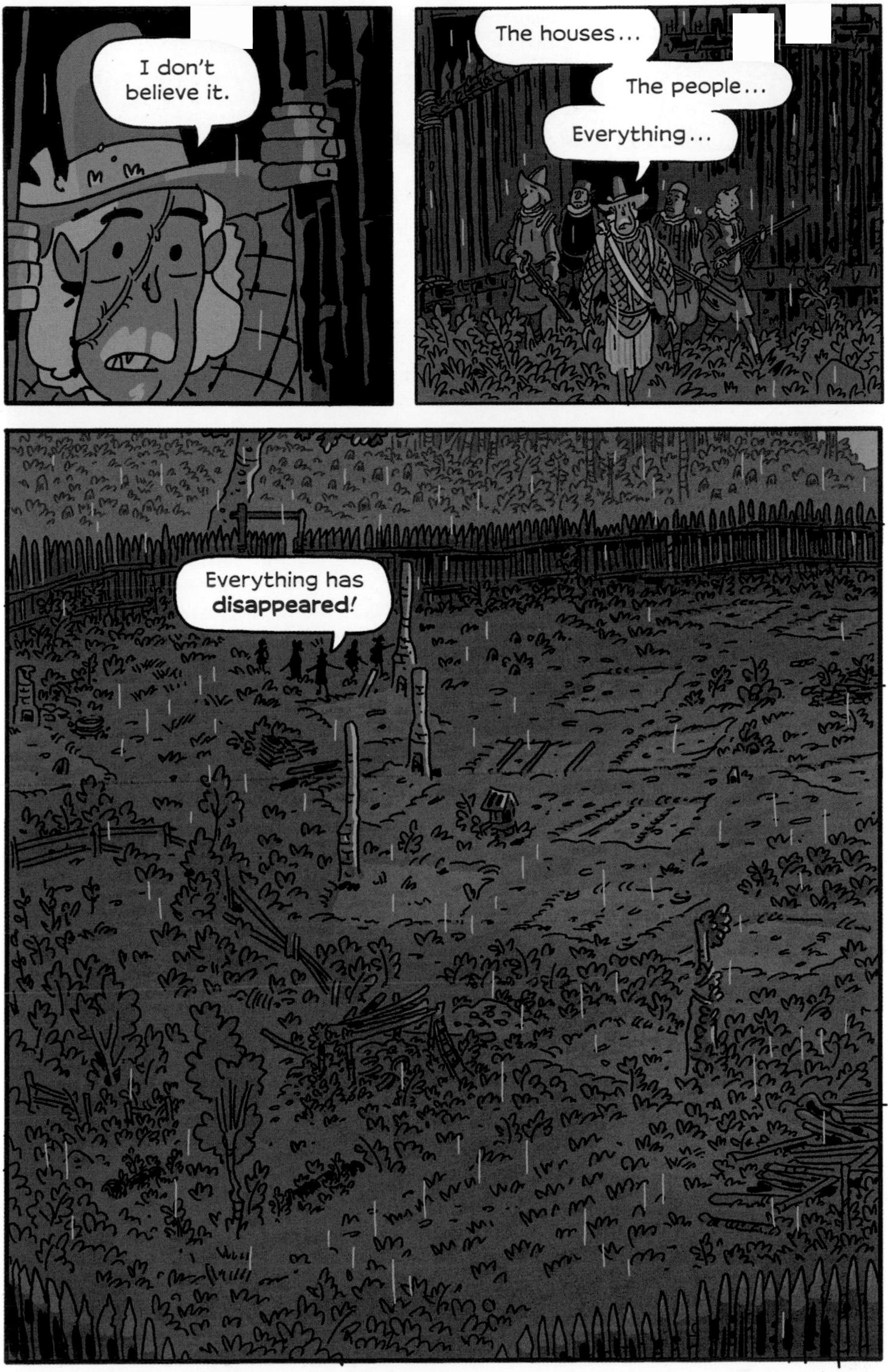
I don't believe it.
The houses...
The people...
Everything...
Everything has **disappeared**!

And thus begins **the greatest unsolved _MYSTERY_ in American history!**

What kind of nonsense are you spewing, Manteo?

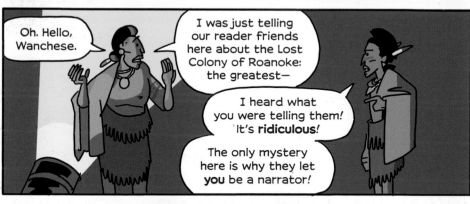

Oh. Hello, Wanchese.

I was just telling our reader friends here about the Lost Colony of Roanoke: the greatest—

I heard what you were telling them! It's **ridiculous!**

The only mystery here is why they let **you** be a narrator!

Because I, Manteo, was **there.**

Yeah, well, I was there, too. And I don't romanticize or exaggerate like you do.

Besides, these readers need a **proper** introduction to the story. They may have never **heard** of Roanoke!

Hmm. That's a good point.

The Lost Colony of Roanoke is important because it was the **first English settlement in North America.**

And because it disappeared*!*

The greatest unsolved mystery in American history!

It's not a mystery at **all**!

Yes, it is*!* Do **you** know what happened to all those colonists?

The evidence **clearly** suggests—

I didn't **ask** what the evidence **"suggests."**

I asked if you **know.**

Look, nobody knows for sure **exactly** what happened, but—

The greatest unsolved mystery in American history, folks!

One hundred English colonists **disappeared**, the only clue a mysterious word carved into a tree...

CROA

But we're going to find out what happened, aren't we, Wanchese?

⇒ *sigh* ⇐

Yes, Manteo. We're going to find out.

The story of the Lost Colony of Roanoke begins on Roanoke itself.

That little place there?

It's not **that** little. It's actually about the same size as Manhattan!

Roanoke Island sits between the barrier islands and the mainland of what is now **North Carolina** in the United States.

It's pretty. I'm glad that the English decided to settle it.

It would be a shame for such beautiful beachfront property to go to waste.

Manteo, Roanoke was **already** settled well before the English arrived.

Sorry, it's easy to forget stuff after four hundred years!

So who lived on Roanoke?

Me!

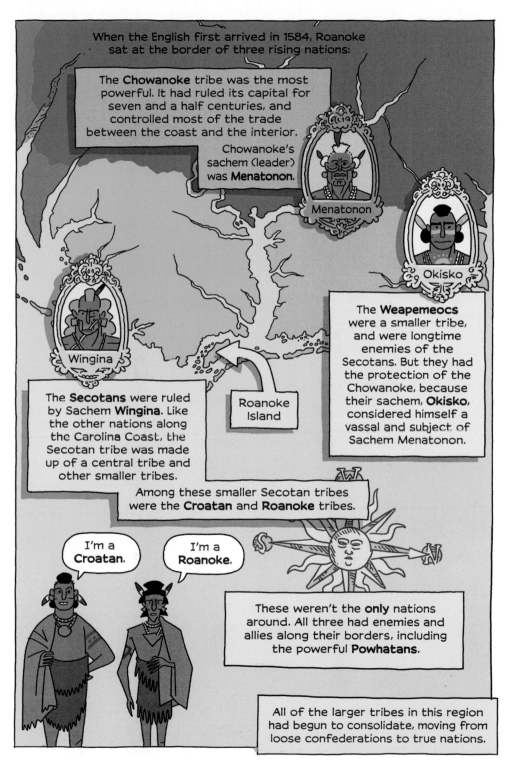

When the English first arrived in 1584, Roanoke sat at the border of three rising nations:

The **Chowanoke** tribe was the most powerful. It had ruled its capital for seven and a half centuries, and controlled most of the trade between the coast and the interior.

Chowanoke's sachem (leader) was **Menatonon**.

Menatonon

Okisko

The **Weapemeocs** were a smaller tribe, and were longtime enemies of the Secotans. But they had the protection of the Chowanoke, because their sachem, **Okisko**, considered himself a vassal and subject of Sachem Menatonon.

Wingina

The **Secotans** were ruled by Sachem **Wingina**. Like the other nations along the Carolina Coast, the Secotan tribe was made up of a central tribe and other smaller tribes.

Roanoke Island

Among these smaller Secotan tribes were the **Croatan** and **Roanoke** tribes.

I'm a **Croatan**.

I'm a **Roanoke**.

These weren't the **only** nations around. All three had enemies and allies along their borders, including the powerful **Powhatans**.

All of the larger tribes in this region had begun to consolidate, moving from loose confederations to true nations.

9

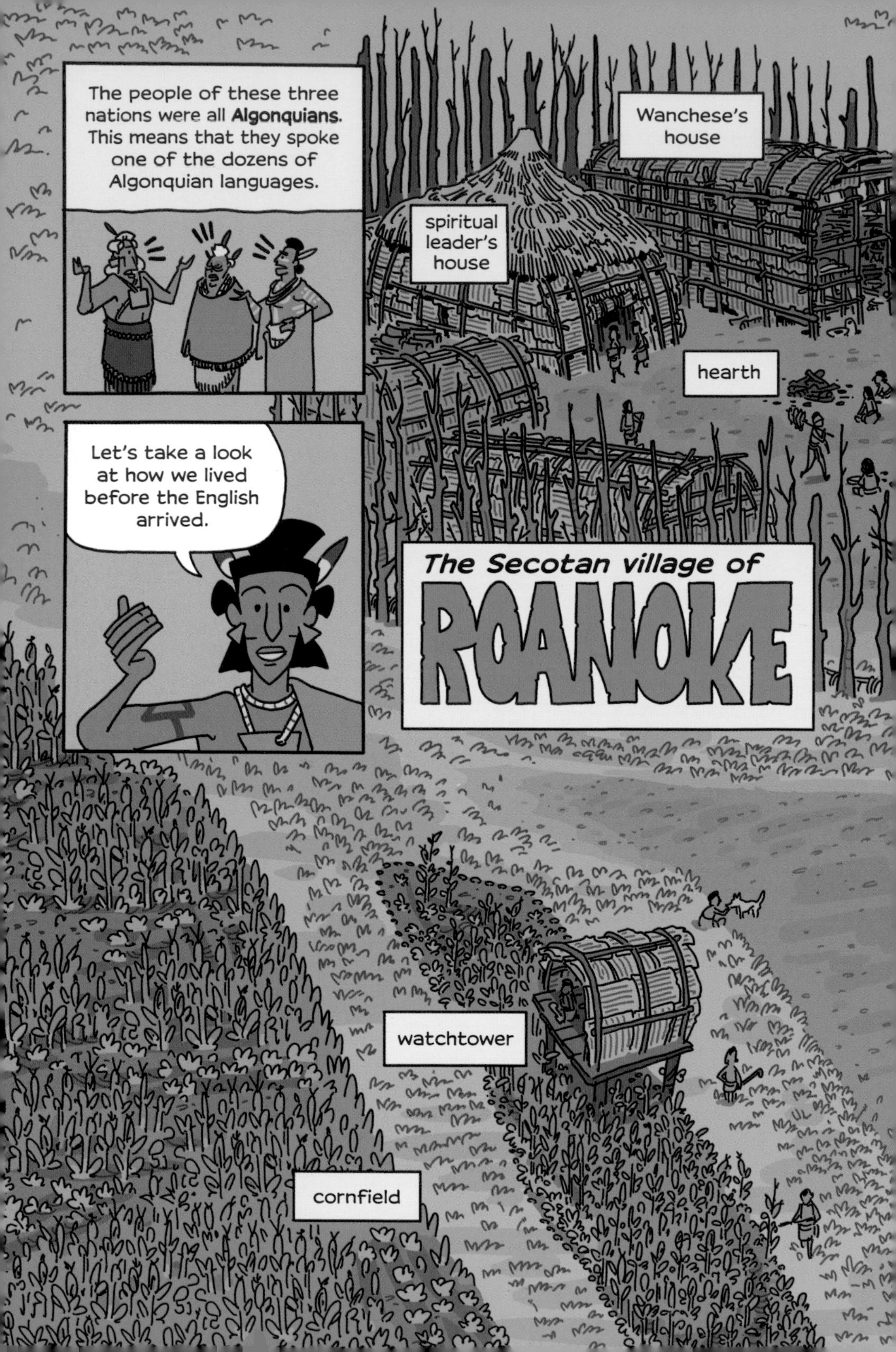

The people of these three nations were all **Algonquians**. This means that they spoke one of the dozens of Algonquian languages.
Let's take a look at how we lived before the English arrived.
Wanchese's house
spiritual leader's house
hearth
The Secotan village of
ROANOKE
watchtower
cornfield

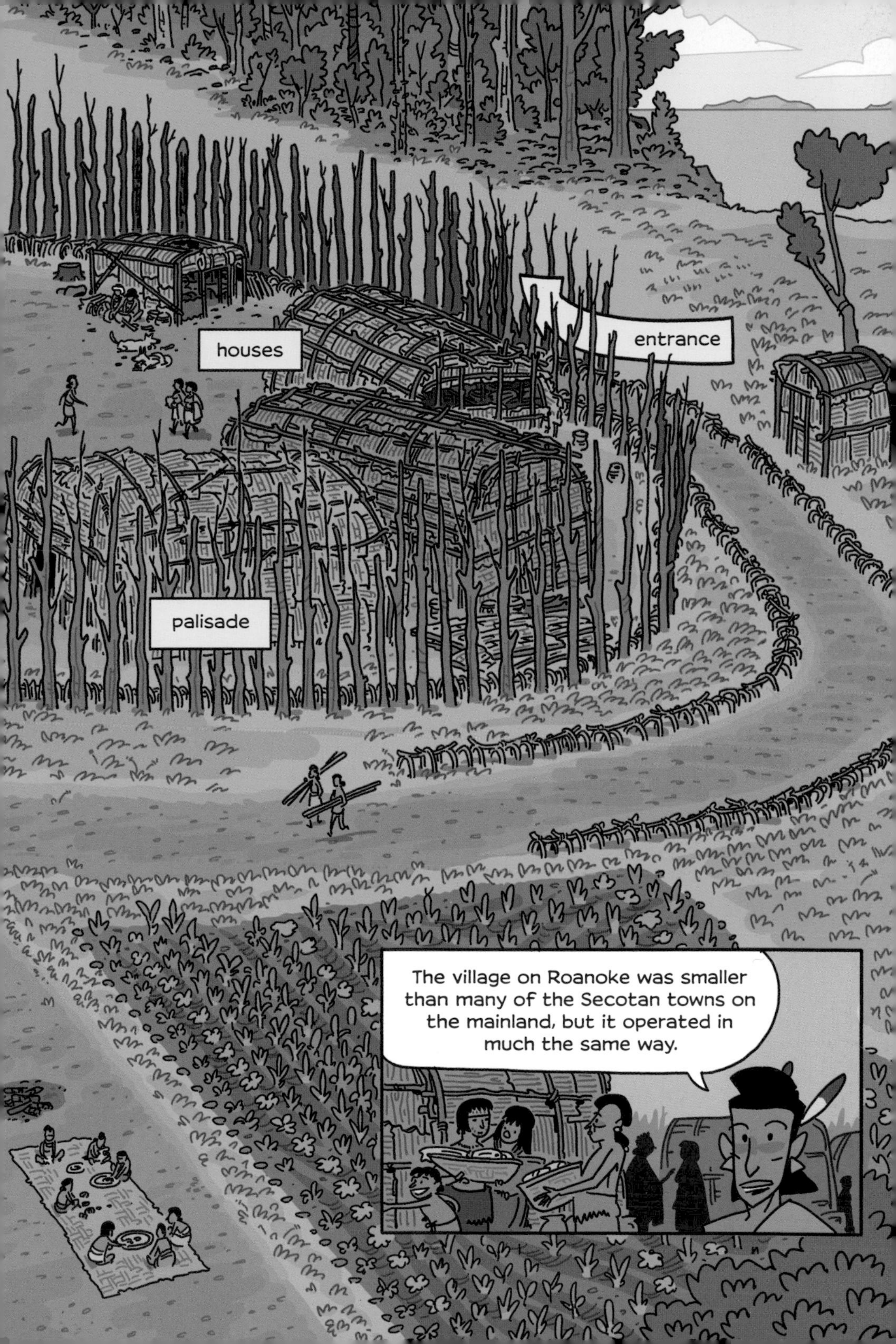
houses
entrance
palisade
The village on Roanoke was smaller than many of the Secotan towns on the mainland, but it operated in much the same way.

We were an **agricultural society**. That means that we relied on **farming**.

We grew **corn** and staggered its planting throughout the year, so that we'd have fresh crops coming up in waves instead of all at once.

We also grew **pumpkins**, **sunflowers**, **gourds**, **beans**, and **tobacco**.

We planted our **beans** and **squash** out in the cornfields* instead of separating the crops the way that the English settlers would.

The bean plants would lock nitrogen in the soil, fertilizing the corn and helping to make it grow more plentifully, and the squash leaves would shade the soil and keep bugs away.

Nearly everyone in the village would help to prepare the soil before each planting.

We would use hoes to dig up all the old stalks and furrow the ground.

We had cleared the trees and brush from the land outside the village to create these fields.

Clearing the land gave us a good view of any enemies that might try to sneak up on us.

*This trio of crops was called "The Three Sisters."

We also relied on other plants besides just the crops that we cultivated in our fields.

We used **grass** to make baskets, mats, and bags...

...**tree bark** to make storage bins for our corn and beans...

...and wild plants such as **sassafras** and **milkweed** to make medicine.

We gathered **nuts** and edible **roots** and **berries** for the winter.

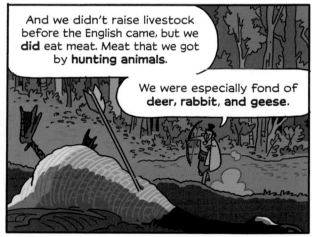

And we didn't raise livestock before the English came, but we **did** eat meat. Meat that we got by **hunting animals**.

We were especially fond of **deer, rabbit, and geese**.

But the most reliable source of protein in our diet was **fish**.

We had all sorts of ways to catch fish!

We would build **weirs**, or fish traps, and gather up the fish that had swum into them.

The fish swim into a maze of reeds that gets narrower and narrower...

...and cannot find their way out of the enclosures (at least not before they're scooped up!).

We would use **nets** made from light-weight wood and woven grass fibers.

And we would **spear** them using rods with barbed points made from fish bones and crab claws.

Sometimes we would fish at night, lighting a fire in the middle of the canoe. The light would attract the fish, and we could scoop them right up!

Hold on a minute!

Isn't setting a fire in a canoe a **really** bad idea?

It would burn a hole right through and we would **sink!**

Not with **our** canoes!

Secotan dugout canoes were made using half of a cypress log. Some of these logs were thirty-five feet long!

The middle of the log was scraped out slowly with seashells and stone tools...

...then burned...

...then scraped, burned, scraped, and burned, again and again until the wood was thin and light enough to be lifted by hand, but strong and hard enough from the constant firing to carry as many as **twenty men**.

Okay, so the wood is already fire-hardened, which makes it much less likely to burn.

I still think starting a fire in the bottom of a canoe seems like a bad idea.

You want to make sure we have fish, don't you?

Night fishing might mean the difference between a meal and going hungry!

Speaking of meals, we would prepare a meal of fish in two different ways.

We would either cook it on a **grill** made out of sticks...

...or we would cook it in a big clay pot with water and vegetables and make a hearty **stew**!

We made our pots using clay. Have you ever made **snakes** out of clay, Manteo?

They were the only thing I was ever good at making!

You just roll the clay into long snaky rods.

The Secotan people would make their pots the same way, **coiling** these clay snake shapes around until the pot was the right size and shape.

We'd keep these pots...

...and all of our stuff...

...in our homes.

The buildings were called **longhouses**.

Bark **wall panels** could be removed for ventilation.

Upper platforms would hold food and supplies.

A mat made from grass or reeds would work as a **door**.

A **hearth** in the middle of the home would be used for cooking and heat.

A wooden **mortar and pestle** would be used to mash grains and herbs for food and medicine.

Firewood could be stored under the sleeping platforms.

Lower platforms covered in furs would serve as beds.

Examining the
LONGHOUSE

Usually, more than one family would live in each longhouse, and these houses also stored the food that we caught, gathered, or harvested.

And though many Secotan towns had palisade walls like the one on Roanoke Island, not all of the buildings would be inside of it.

If a town had more people than little Roanoke, the houses of the town's civic leader, its councillors, and its spiritual leaders would be inside the walls, but most of the others would have houses outside.

There were plenty of Secotan towns in which **none** of the buildings were inside a palisade.

These towns were often farther from the border with the other nations, and safer from attack.

The spiritual leaders of a town were called **kwiocusuks**, and the buildings in which they lived and prayed were called **quiocosins**. If the town was large enough to have a civic leader (called **werowances** if men, **weroansquas** if women), their remains would be kept in the quiocosins until they could be ceremonially buried.

Spiritual connections were an important part of our daily lives. We believed that we must pray and hold ceremonies in order to have a good harvest, avoid disaster, and show our gratitude for the world in which we lived.

Ritual dances

Praying

Ceremonial feasts

Algonquian towns and cities would have two types of kwiocusuk:

Flattened woodpecker!

Old men, chosen for their wisdom and knowledge, led the rituals for the town and were responsible for the tribe's spiritual ceremonies.

They were in charge of feasts, fasts, burials, sacrifices, and dances.

Younger men, chosen for their connection to the spirit world, would intercede in non-ceremonial daily problems such as sickness or calamity.

They served as prophets and operated as town doctors, exorcists, and councillors.

The town's **werowance** was a hereditary office. The leader's parent, grandparent, or aunt or uncle would have been the werowance before them.

A town's werowance might be the subject of a more powerful regional werowance...

...who was himself a subject of the **sachem**.

Werowances and sachems were elevated positions, but they did not make laws or issue commands.

They would discuss things with a council, and decisions were made by consensus (everyone agreeing to a course of action).

This included when and how to go to **war**.

War for the Algonquian nations was a different concept than it was for the English settlers.

It was very rare that there would be set battles on battlefields. Usually, one party would conduct a raid on another.

Sometimes these would be skirmishes over territorial disputes on the border, but mostly they were **reprisals**.

If a person from one tribe wronged a person from another...

Ha-ha! I stole all your arrows!

...then the tribe of the person who was wronged might go to **war** against the tribe of the person who had done the wrong.

Ha-ha! Now we stole all of **your** arrows!

⇒ *sigh* ⇐ I guess that's fair.

War was often seen as a way to get **justice**, and justice was seen as **balance** between tribes.

Once balance was restored, the war was over.

So we farmed, prayed, fought, hunted, made things, traveled, and were pretty content. We lived in a bountiful land and even though things were changing...

...things are **always** changing...

...we felt like we had a pretty good handle on the world and **thought** we knew what we could expect of our lives.

But then **everything** changed.

On July 4, 1584, English ships arrived at Roanoke Island.

But where did these ships come from?

Why were they here?

Who sent them?

To learn **that**, we have to **leave** Roanoke and go all the way across the Atlantic Ocean to the island nation of **England**...

...and meet **England's** sachem.

QUEEN ELIZABETH I

1533 — 1603

Holy moly! Look at those jacked-up arms!

Those are just her **sleeves**, Manteo!

When Elizabeth first began her reign as queen, England was a fairly insignificant island.

By the end of her forty-four years ruling the country, it was emerging as a world power.

Elizabeth **loved** to flirt. If you were a handsome young courtier and you were good at flirting with the queen, there was no limit to your opportunities!

This was harder than it might sound. The queen was extremely jealous and also her teeth were rotten because she used honey for toothpaste.

Take him away!

But all I did was offer you a breath mint!

So how did Elizabeth help England become an important country?

It mostly boils down to **religion**.

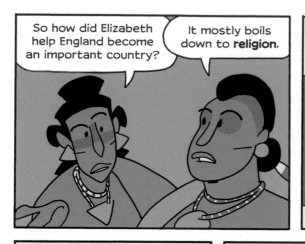

During Elizabeth's time, there were two types of Christians that hated each other:

You're a heretic and if I have **my** way you'll burn at the stake!

Protestants and **Catholics**.

Elizabeth, who was Protestant, inherited the throne from her sister, who had been Catholic.

She decided to make England a **Protestant** country.

This put England on a collision course with Spain. Spain was the most powerful nation in Europe, and it was a **Catholic** country.

Watch it!

The king of Spain (and ruler of the vast Spanish Empire) was Philip II.

He was a staunch Catholic and considered it his sacred duty to defend Catholicism against any threats...

...and he considered Elizabeth a threat.

Philip plotted with Elizabeth's cousin, **Mary**, Queen of Scots. Mary was Catholic and Philip wanted **her** to be the queen of England.

But Elizabeth found out and had Mary executed.

My poor, dear cousin!

After the executioner cut off Mary's head, he held it up high for the crowd to see. Unfortunately, Mary had been wearing a wig, and the head fell right out.

Oops.

Philip had been playing a long game, hoping to see England eventually return to Catholicism, but Mary's death meant he would have to make other plans.

Elizabeth had known for years that Philip wanted to install a Catholic monarch on England's throne. If he couldn't do that, he might try to conquer England and make it part of the Spanish Empire itself.

So even though England and Spain were **technically** at peace, Queen Elizabeth encouraged some very un-peaceful activities.

Oh boy oh boy oh boy!

We're going to talk about the **pirates** now, aren't we?

Shiver me timbers! Avast, ye swabs!

≥sigh≤

THE SPANISH EMPIRE

The Spanish Empire was one of the largest, richest, and most powerful empires in history.

Based in Spain, Philip controlled parts of Europe, Asia, Africa, and, most important, the Americas.

By the 1580s, Spain had already spent decades plundering the wealth of the New World. As many as eight million Americans were killed in war, at work, or by the new diseases carried by the Spanish, and those who survived were made to convert to Catholicism and were often forced to work in Spain's silver mines.

In addition to mining, the Spanish would melt down gold taken from the Aztecs and the Incas.

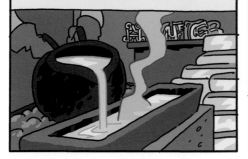

Every year they would have thousands upon thousands of pounds of gold and silver to send back to Spain.

This gold made Spain so rich that no other country could hope to compete with it. Their armies were better paid and better equipped than anyone else's, and they could afford to build hundreds of huge ships called **galleons**.

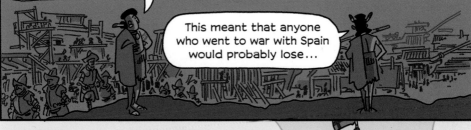

This meant that anyone who went to war with Spain would probably lose...

...including **England**.

But all that treasure had to get from the Americas to Spain, and to do that, it had to cross the ocean...

...and the ocean can be a **dangerous** place.

What made it especially dangerous to Spanish ships were English **privateers**.

Is a privateer the same thing as a **pirate**?

Well... ...sort of.

Elizabeth would give letters saying that it was legal to attack Spanish ships and steal whatever was on board to merchants whose ships had been confiscated by the Spanish.

But these "privateers" are **only** allowed to plunder as much money as they **lost**.

We just want our property back... It's not like we're **pirates**.

A portion of everything plundered went to the Queen. Easy money! Pretty soon the idea of simply recouping losses wasn't enough, and Elizabeth began giving privateering licenses to **anyone** who might bring treasure in.

We're still not **pirates**... We don't attack just **anyone**, only those dastardly **Spaniards**.

Really, though, the temptation of plunder was too strong, and most privateers would attack **anybody** they **encountered**.

I'm French, and my ship was raided!

I'm Dutch, and my ship was raided!

I'm **English**, and **my** ship was raided!

Okay, **maybe** we're pirates...

At first, privateers stuck to the English Channel and other European waters, attacking small Spanish merchants.

Hey, wait a second!

The Spanish have **huge** galleons, right? Big floating towns packed to the brim with tons and tons of **treasure** coming from the Americas?

Yep.

And so huge fleets of privateers were assembled, financed by investors and led by glory-seeking English gentlemen low on cash, and to the Americas they went.

The privateers wreaked unimaginable damage on the Spanish, capturing treasure or sinking treasure ships. Spain's steady source of income was suddenly not so steady!

Many men who would go on to become prominent figures in English politics and history got their start as privateers...

...and few would rise with such panache as **Sir Walter Raleigh**, universally acknowledged as the sexiest dude in 1580s England.

That's a weird thing for people to universally acknowledge.

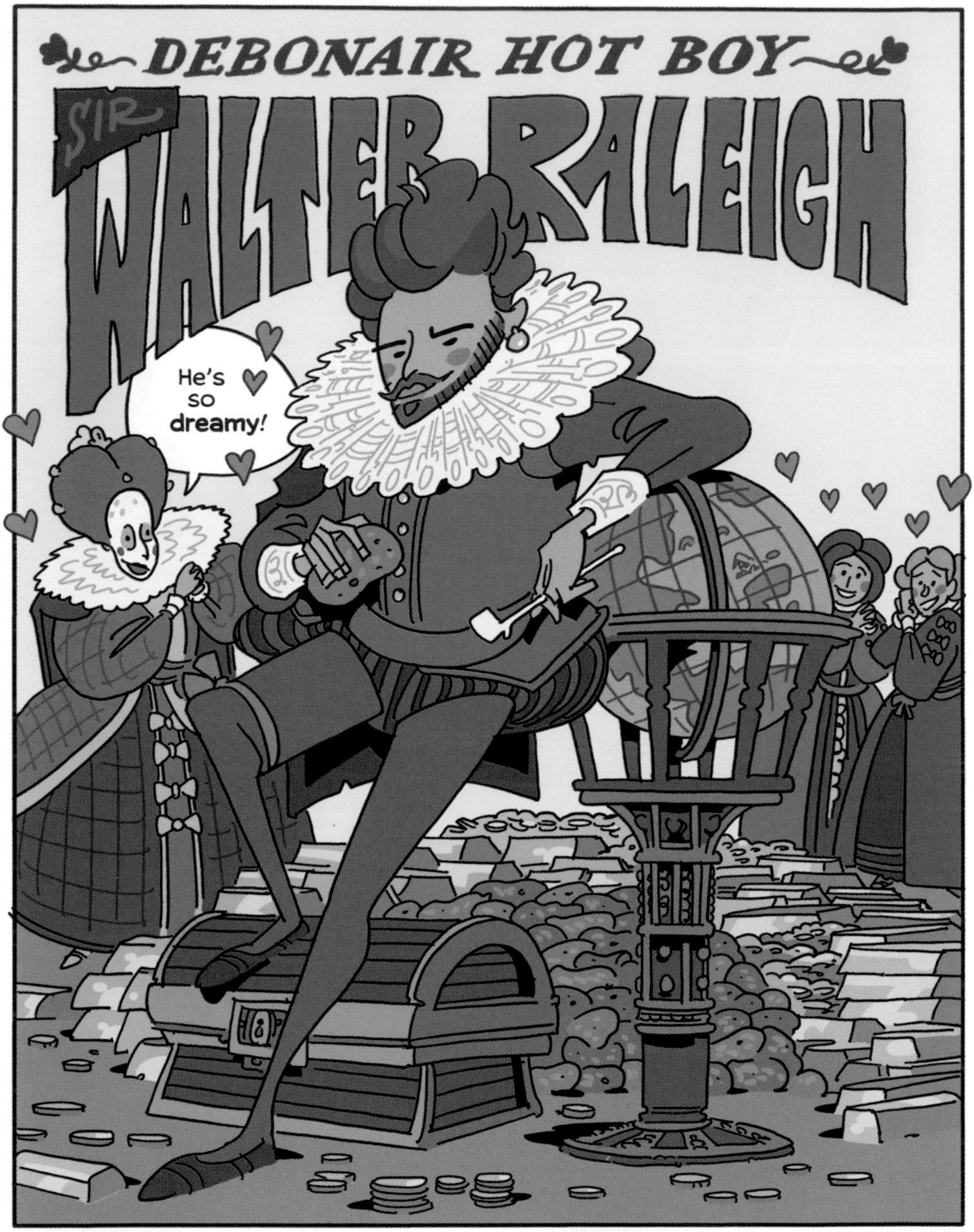
DEBONAIR HOT BOY
SIR WALTER RALEIGH
He's so **dreamy**!

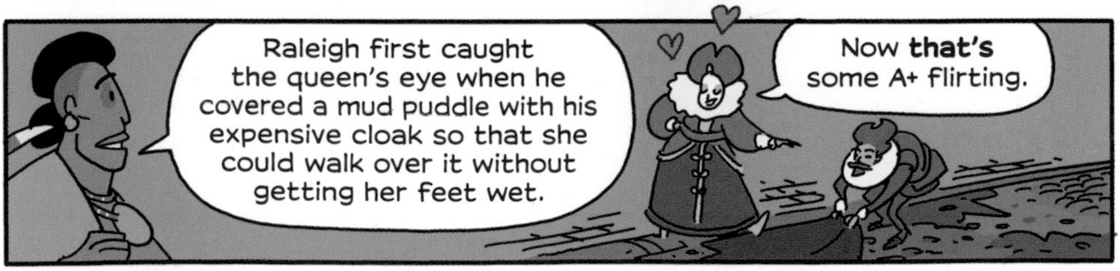
Raleigh first caught the queen's eye when he covered a mud puddle with his expensive cloak so that she could walk over it without getting her feet wet.
Now **that's** some A+ flirting.

Since the queen had no intention of marrying anyone, she had to find **other** ways to show her affection.

Raleigh, dear, you're simply **delicious**.

I've got a **present** for you!

What is it, Walt?

It's a **patent**! The queen has given me the exclusive rights to explore, colonize, and rule over any lands that don't have a Christian king!

Hope you like it, darling. And don't you go marrying any of my friends, or I'll lock you up!*

He did, and she did!

Sir Walter was excited about starting a colony in North America, but **not** because he expected the land to become a new home for English settlers or a source of crops and trade goods. He wanted it for only one reason...

We'll make a **base** in North America from which to launch our **privateering raids** against the Spanish!

Hang on a minute, Manteo.

So we're talking almost the entire eastern coastline of what will eventually become the United States and Canada, untold riches in resources...

...and the **only** thing Raleigh cared about was having a **base** from which to launch his pirate ships?

That seems, well, **shortsighted**, even for the English!

Shortsighted is **right**, Wanchese. This obsession with privateering is not only what will **create** the Lost Colony of Roanoke, but it might have been the **cause** of its **downfall**!

I **was** wondering why we were spending so much time on this privateering stuff.

I think we ought to get back to Roanoke. After all, **that's** what this story is about!

Quite a few people had explored the North American coastline and it was clear to everyone that the best place to build a self-sufficient colony was the **Chesapeake Bay**, in what is now Maryland, Virginia, and Delaware.

So that's where Raleigh decided to send his settlers?

Nope. It was too far from Spanish shipping. Raleigh wanted to be as close to Spanish territory as was safe.

Spain had a fort in what would become **South Carolina**, so Raleigh decided to put his settlement just a little bit north, in what would become **North Carolina**.

Putting together a colony would be a long and expensive task, but Raleigh's patent gave him only seven years to do it.

I'll launch a small expedition while I'm getting everything together.

Raleigh appointed two men to lead the expedition:

Philip Amadas

Arthur Barlowe

Amadas and Barlowe **weren't** setting up a colony. They were scouting for the colony that would come later.

Amadas and Barlowe dropped anchor just a little east of Roanoke Island, next to smaller **Hatteras Island**.

Within a week, a few dozen Secotans rowed to Hatteras to hold court with the newcomers.

Their leader was **Granganimeo**, brother of Sachem Wingina and werowance of the Secotan town on the mainland across from Roanoke Island.

Amadas and Barlowe rowed out with the ship's pilot and a few armed guards to join Granganimeo on the beach.

Granganimeo, Amadas, and Barlowe hit it off. The werowance gave a big speech and the Englishmen gave him a tin plate that Granganimeo made into an armored necklace.

Come on, shoot me! It'll bounce right off.

I'd **really** rather not, boss.

In exchange for metal goods such as teapots, axes, and knives, the Secotans offered up a huge amount of valuable animal skins.

Amadas, Barlowe, and their crew spent a few very pleasant weeks among the Secotans.

Wanchese! Wanchese!

Look who they're talking to!

Yeah, Manteo, they're talking to **us**.

This is so weird. Can we hear us?

Manteo! Manteo, it's me, Manteo!

Quit fooling around, Manteo. We've got a lot of history to cover...

Hey! What are you doing?!

I've never seen what my own butt looks like!

We're **narrators**, Manteo! A very **dignified** position!

How is using history to see your own butt undignified?

Barlowe kept a detailed account of what he saw in Roanoke and some of the nearby towns.

He loved everything about the Carolina coast, especially how inviting he thought it would be to the English when they came to settle.

The natives here are friendly and helpful...

...the land is incredibly fertile and will yield no end of rich crops...

...there is an endless supply of fish and animals to hunt...

...and best of all, **no one** is **using** this land!

England colonizing Roanoke? Why, it would be the **easiest** thing in the world!

But Wanchese, everything Barlowe just said was **wrong**!

Oh?

Yeah! We were helpful and friendly because we thought that they were **temporary** visitors who would obey our customs and laws.

And the land isn't "incredibly fertile," at least not on Roanoke Island.

The island soil is **okay** for growing crops, but it isn't **great**. If we didn't rotate our fields each year, it would be depleted in no time!

There's a lot of game to hunt and fish to catch, but it's hard work, and not consistent, and if we do it too much in one place, we drive those creatures away.

And I'm pretty darn sure that someone **is** using the land!

Telling people that settling here is going to be easy seems like asking for trouble.

The people who come won't be prepared for the hardships that they'll face, especially if they try to grow their crops the English way!

Is Barlowe **lying** in his report, or is he foolish and naive?

A little of both. Barlowe wasn't exactly **lying**. He was **exaggerating**.

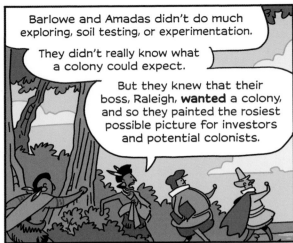

Barlowe and Amadas didn't do much exploring, soil testing, or experimentation.

They didn't really know what a colony could expect.

But they knew that their boss, Raleigh, **wanted** a colony, and so they painted the rosiest possible picture for investors and potential colonists.

Once the Englishmen felt that they had learned enough to convince people that colonizing Roanoke would be a good idea, they decided to head back to England.

And they decided to bring a couple of clever, handsome, brave explorers along with them, **didn't** they?

MANTEO & WANCHESE'S

Daring expedition into the heart of exotic

ENGLAND!

When Amadas and Barlowe left, we volunteered to leave with them.

We wanted to see the land that these strange visitors had come from for ourselves.

If they were to be **friends**, I wanted to know all about them!

If they were to be **enemies**, **I** wanted to know all about them!

England was like nothing we had ever seen before.

These buildings! The clothes! It's extraordinary!

Some have so much, while others have so little! It's **barbaric!**

We may even have been presented to Queen Elizabeth.

Oh, my! I hope they teach you fine fellows how to **flirt** in America.

And we were introduced to **Thomas Harriot**, a mathematician who taught us English, and to whom we taught Algonquian.

MOCCASIN

SKUNK PECAN

HICKORY

RACCOON

SQUASH

TOMAHAWK

OPOSSUM

Now, Thomas, there are all **sorts** of Algonquian words that have no English equivalent.

We spent a lot of time with Harriot, and taught him all about Secotan culture, religion, and customs.

When we returned to America, he planned to come with us.

I want to see the land that you strange visitors have come from for myself!

I know the feeling, pal.

Our presence in England helped to bolster excitement for Raleigh's venture. The plans for colonizing Roanoke were underway!

The chief planners were a couple of guys who were both named **Richard Hakluyt**.

Hi, I'm Richard Hakluyt.

(They were cousins.)

The Hakluyts had studied the colonies that Spain, France, and Portugal had established in the Americas.

We have really good ideas for how to start **and** maintain a colony that will thrive and benefit England.

First: our English sailors don't know math, so they can't navigate! We have to rely on Spanish or Portuguese navigators.

Our colleges need to start teaching **math**!

You can thank the Hakluyts for math class!

Second: we need to build our own ships.

America has plenty of timber, so setting up shipyards there will give England a strong navy **and** help the colonies pay for **themselves**!

Third: if we let these new "corporations" be in charge of colonization, long-term prosperity will **always** be sacrificed for short-term profits for shareholders.

The government should be in charge, **not** businessmen!

Last, and most important of **all**: we **must** treat the **natives** with **patience** and **respect**!

Our colonists won't be able to survive without the locals' guidance.

If we use violence as freely as we have in our other colonies, we'll lose their friendship, and the colony will be

doomed!

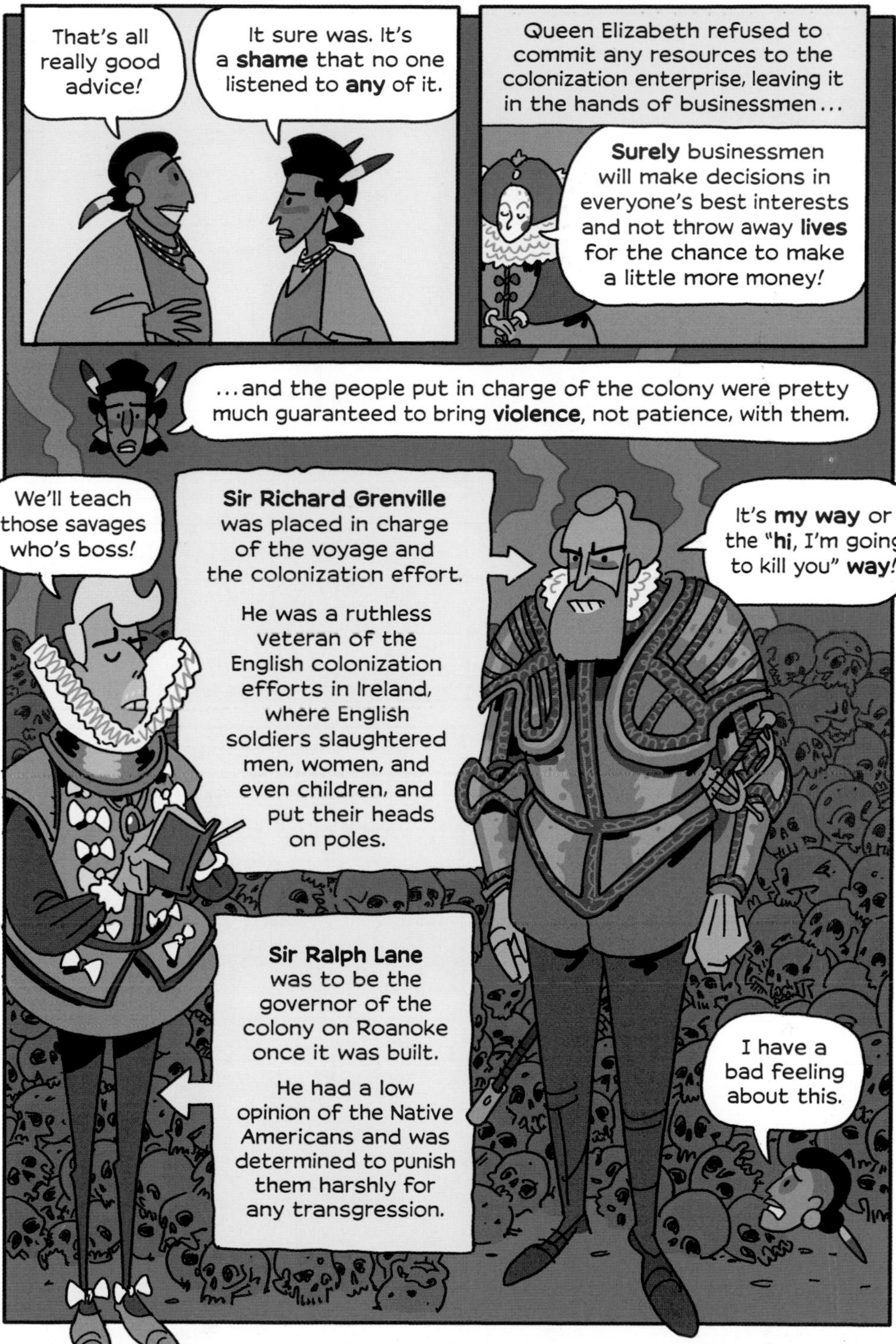
That's all really good advice!
It sure was. It's a **shame** that no one listened to **any** of it.
Queen Elizabeth refused to commit any resources to the colonization enterprise, leaving it in the hands of businessmen...
Surely businessmen will make decisions in everyone's best interests and not throw away **lives** for the chance to make a little more money!
...and the people put in charge of the colony were pretty much guaranteed to bring **violence**, not patience, with them.
We'll teach those savages who's boss!
Sir Richard Grenville was placed in charge of the voyage and the colonization effort.
He was a ruthless veteran of the English colonization efforts in Ireland, where English soldiers slaughtered men, women, and even children, and put their heads on poles.
It's **my way** or the "**hi**, I'm going to kill you" **way**!
Sir Ralph Lane was to be the governor of the colony on Roanoke once it was built.
He had a low opinion of the Native Americans and was determined to punish them harshly for any transgression.
I have a bad feeling about this.

Also part of the expedition was Manteo's friend **Thomas Harriot**, who planned to study the American people.

With him was **John White**, an artist who would make detailed paintings of them.

Those guys are **really** ill-suited to running a new colony in America.

I have a bad feeling about this.

See? **These** guys know what's up.

The rest of the colonists were either Ralph Lane's upper-crust friends, to whom he gave so many military titles he was told he couldn't do that anymore...

But this is my favorite part of being governor!

You can still make **me** a general, right?

...mineral experts who would be testing metals and the soil looking for gold, silver, iron, copper, and tin...

...and the poor people, war veterans, and artisans who'd do all the work.

Some of us were **forced** to go!

With enough supplies to last them for a year, the colonists set off with five ships and a handful of pinnaces and other small support boats.

We were on board *Tyger!*

Elizabeth

Red Lion

Tyger

Roebuck

Dorothy

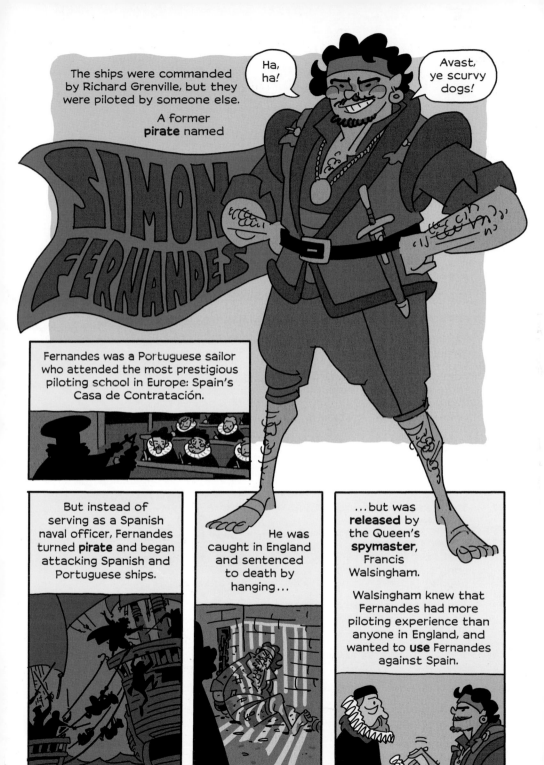

The ships were commanded by Richard Grenville, but they were piloted by someone else.

A former **pirate** named

SIMON FERNANDES

Ha, ha!

Avast, ye scurvy dogs!

Fernandes was a Portuguese sailor who attended the most prestigious piloting school in Europe: Spain's Casa de Contratación.

But instead of serving as a Spanish naval officer, Fernandes turned **pirate** and began attacking Spanish and Portuguese ships.

He was caught in England and sentenced to death by hanging...

...but was **released** by the Queen's **spymaster**, Francis Walsingham.

Walsingham knew that Fernandes had more piloting experience than anyone in England, and wanted to **use** Fernandes against Spain.

Getting to know

TYGER

1 - The big vertical poles are the **masts**.

2 - The horizontal poles from which the sails hang are the **yards**.

3 - The front of the ship is called the **bow**.

4 - The back of the ship is called the **stern**.

5 - If you're facing forward, the left side of the ship is **port**, the right **starboard**.

6 - The parts of the ship that you can walk on are the **decks**.

7 - Crewmen sleep on hammocks in the **forecastle** (pronounced "foxel").

8 - Cannons aboard a ship are called **guns**. These require a gun crew to load and fire them.

9 - Some sailing ships also use long oars for movement when there is not enough wind. These types of ships are called galleys or galleasses. Even though English ships rarely used oars, Grenville converted *Tyger* to a **galleass**.

10 - The **tops** give lookouts the chance to spot land, or ships belonging to the enemy.

11 - The **captain's cabin** is located at the stern, and has big windows.

12 - The **hold** is where supplies and food were stored.

13 - **Shrouds** are ropes that keep the masts upright and which can be used as ladders.

14 - The bottom of the ship is weighed down by **ballast** to keep it from tipping over.

15 - The long pole extending off the bow is the **bowsprit**.

16 - Spare sailcloth, rope, and wood are stored in the **forepeak**.

17 - There were no ship's wheels in the 1580s. *Tyger* was steered with a long pole attached to the rudder called a **tiller**.

18 - There are no bathrooms. You just go off the railing. The whole sea is your toilet!

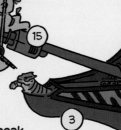

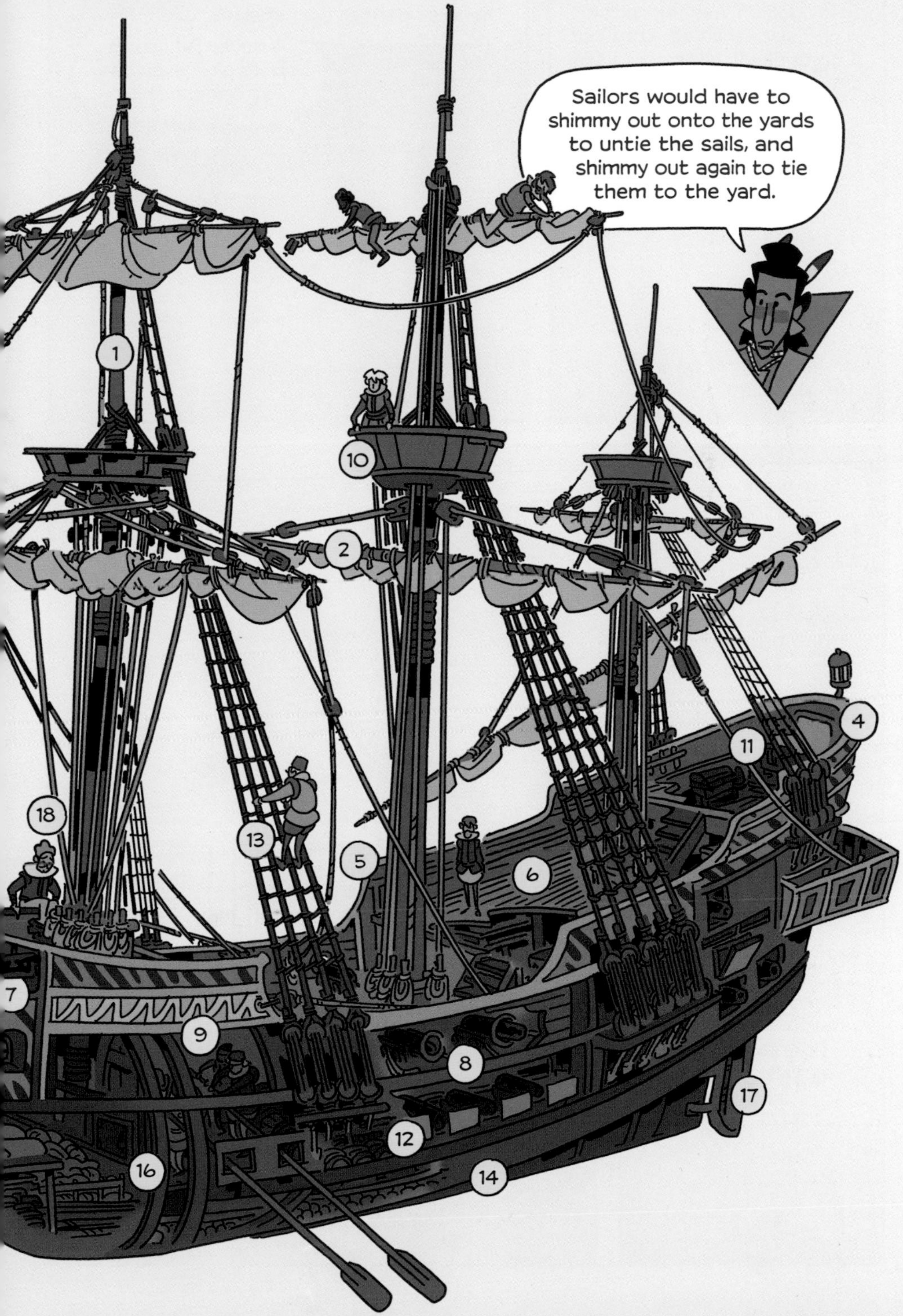
Sailors would have to shimmy out onto the yards to untie the sails, and shimmy out again to tie them to the yard.
1
10
2
4
11
18
13
5
6
7
9
8
17
12
16
14

Navigation was imprecise in the sixteenth century, but a competent pilot could still direct a ship reasonably well.

Even so, there were two big dangers that awaited *Tyger* and its companion ships.

The first danger was **storms**.

A powerful storm could sink even the strongest ship.

One week into the voyage, a storm destroyed one of the pinnaces and scattered the fleet.

Tyger had to make the long Atlantic crossing by itself.

Grenville had planned a rendezvous for the fleet in case they were separated: **Puerto Rico**, in Spanish-controlled waters.

The other ships in the fleet weren't there yet, but Grenville kept his eyes sharp for sails. And not just for his comrades, but for Spanish treasure galleons.

This was the other great danger to the colony fleet:

The temptation to hunt for **prizes**!

That's a **danger**? I thought that was the whole **point** of the Roanoke colony!

It **was** the whole point. Which is the **problem**.

The colony was only there to facilitate privateering...

...but by prioritizing privateering over the needs of the colony, the people in charge sowed the seeds for its **certain doom**!

A colony was a **long-term** investment. **Eventually** it would yield valuable exotic crops and trade goods provided by Natives.

But a captured Spanish ship meant **immediate** money. The ship itself was valuable, as was its cargo and, in some cases, the treasure it carried.

The people in charge of the Roanoke colony would put their supplies, men, and schedule at risk if there was even the slightest chance of capturing one.

Grenville **took** that risk. He waited in the Caribbean for three weeks while his men built a new pinnace, and while there he attacked and captured two Spanish ships.

By the time the ship *Elizabeth* arrived at the rendezvous, Grenville had *Tyger*, two captured Spanish ships, and his new pinnace.

Good.

I'm sick of waiting for the others. Time to make our way up to Roanoke!

Roanoke Island is protected from the Atlantic Ocean by sandbanks and small barrier islands.

It would be impossible for a Spanish force to bring their large ships in close enough to land troops or shoot cannons.

That's why Raleigh thought it would be a good privateering base!

Unfortunately for the Roanoke colonists, the narrow, shallow channels leading through the islands were too small for the English ships, too.

Uh-oh.

Tyger ran aground on a sandbar.

Water poured through its hull and waves battered it like giant fists.

Eventually, the force of the waves, the changing tide, and the efforts of the crew got *Tyger* off the sandbar, and the crew was able to make repairs on a beach.

But most of the colony's food, gunpowder, and other stores had been **ruined** by the seawater.

The crew, in the pinnace, took soundings (depth measurements) of all of the channels leading from the ocean to Roanoke.

While the other small support boats could get through easily enough, the sounders found **no** path through which the larger ships could travel.

Raleigh's plan to use Roanoke as a base in which privateer ships could safely hide from the Spanish was **impossible**.

Grenville was **furious** at Simon Fernandes. As the pilot of *Tyger*, Fernandes was held responsible for the accident.

Useless, treacherous, incompetent **oaf!**

Then again, Grenville was **always** furious at **everybody**.

Useless, treacherous, incompetent **oafs!**

Grenville did not play well with others.

Remember, it's **my way** or the "**hi**, I'm going to kill you" **way!**

Leadership duties were **supposed** to be divided among the expedition's leaders:

Philip Amadas was vice admiral and would stay to command the fleet in colonial waters.

Ralph Lane was in charge of the men.

High marshal Thomas Cavendish had the power to veto Grenville's decisions.

There wasn't a clear chain of command.

In reality, Grenville refused to allow anyone to wield any control whatsoever.

He was a tyrant!

If any of the others tried to **use** the legal power of their position in the company, or even make a **suggestion** about what the fleet should do, Grenville would threaten to have them **executed**!

The whole me-killing-people-when-I-don't-get-my-way thing?

That's not just **talk**!

Having a stubborn, tyrannical, hot-tempered, and inexperienced leader like Grenville would make life miserable for everyone.

It would also lead to some **serious** problems with the Secotan Natives.

Grenville sent **me** and a couple of his men to Roanoke to get word to Sachem Wingina that we had arrived.

And it wasn't just the ships that had come up from Puerto Rico. Two other ships from the scattered fleet had also found their way to the Carolina waters.

Grenville and the other colonists went to visit the sachem, and were given a grand reception.

They also visited other Secotan towns along the water. One such town, Aquascocock, was nervous having these ruffled, smelly foreigners showing up at their homes uninvited, expecting the Natives to feed and entertain them.

After they left, Grenville found that a silver cup was missing.

Maybe somebody dropped it, boss.

I bet those dirty, thieving **Natives** stole it!

Excuse me?!

I was starting to think that these English settlers were bad news.

Captain Amadas, take a bunch of men back to the village and **get that cup back.**

Amadas took eleven men back to Aquascocock and demanded the return of the missing cup.

Look, I get that you're real worked up over this cup, but **we don't have it.**

Maybe somebody dropped it.

Well, maybe somebody "dropped" a whole bunch of **fire** on your cruddy little town.

Amadas and his men burned down the town and set fire to its fields of crops.

Grenville believed that if the colonists were to allow any slight (real or imagined) to go unpunished, it would be a sign of **weakness**.

If the colonists were seen as weak, he reasoned, then there would be nothing to keep the Natives from killing them and taking their stuff.

Hey, when **I** see weakness, I kill people and take their stuff, so that's going to shape my worldview.

Speaking of killing people and taking their stuff, Grenville also took a party north to a Weapemeoc village.

Amadas and Barlowe had been attacked by Weapemeocs during their first expedition...

...a detail they **left out** of their report so that investors wouldn't worry...

...and Grenville figured **revenge** was **good policy**.

He killed twenty Weapemeocs and raided their village, taking food and captives...

...captives who he gave to Sachem Wingina's brother, Werowance Granganimeo.

I guess the enemy of my enemies is my...friend?

Grenville wanted the Secotans to know that even though he wouldn't hesitate to kill them, he was "on their side."

I tried to tell Granganimeo that the settlers were **bad news**.

But **I** loved the settlers and thought we could learn a lot from them.

I convinced Granganimeo to grant the Englishmen permission to settle on Roanoke.

Grenville may have hated to allow other people to make decisions, and he may have hated Ralph Lane...

May have? Buddy, there's no question about it!

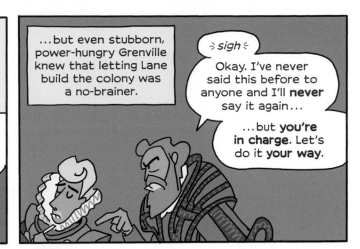

...but even stubborn, power-hungry Grenville knew that letting Lane build the colony was a no-brainer.

⇒ *sigh* ⇐

Okay. I've never said this before to anyone and I'll **never** say it again...

...but **you're in charge.** Let's do it **your way.**

Lane was an expert at building forts and fortifications.

He had constructed two forts in Spanish waters just weeks earlier while the men aboard *Tyger* awaited the rest of the fleet.

It took a lot of time to prepare the land for Lane's Roanoke fort. The men were put to work cutting down trees (and using them to make lumber), clearing the brush, and digging trenches for the earthworks.

The ships couldn't reach the island to unload tools and supplies, and jumping off the longboats and pinnaces onto the bank meant that you were always getting your supplies, clothes, and shoes wet.

Lane built a **jetty** to make the unloading easier.

Eventually, the advance work was done, and the fort could be built.

51

THE FIRST ENGLISH COLONY on ROANOKE

under Governor Ralph Lane, 1585

Officers in the company had their own small **houses** so that they didn't have to sleep beside their men.

Trees were **cut down** to make the approach to the fort visible, and to supply wood for building.

A small **garden** gave the colonists a way to test new crops.

Settlers could enter the fort through a guarded wooden **gate**.

A **forge** was built so that colonists could make nails and do repairs on other metal tools. The fires for the forge were incredibly hot, so it was kept separate to protect the other flammable buildings.

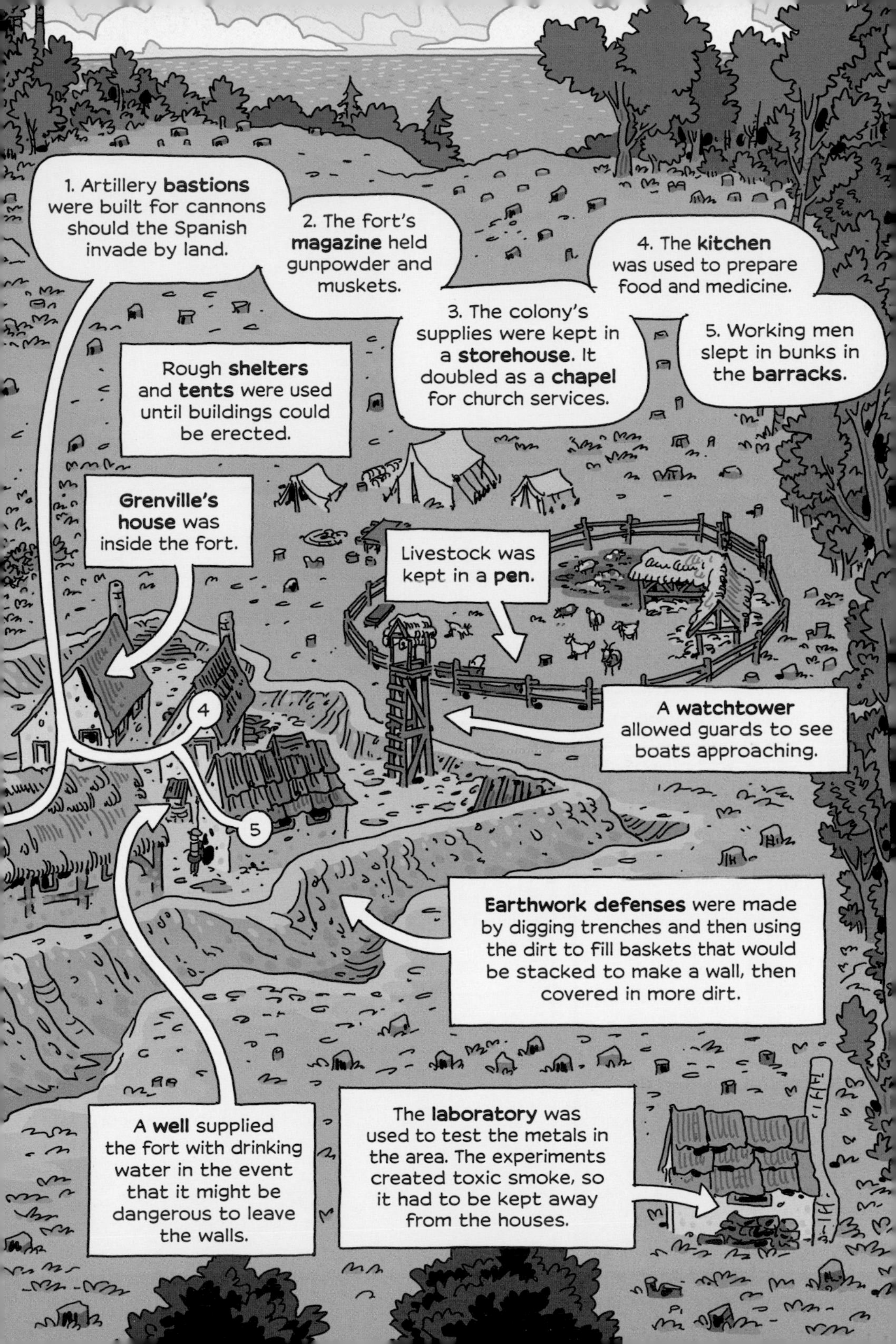
1. Artillery **bastions** were built for cannons should the Spanish invade by land.
2. The fort's **magazine** held gunpowder and muskets.
3. The colony's supplies were kept in a **storehouse**. It doubled as a **chapel** for church services.
4. The **kitchen** was used to prepare food and medicine.
5. Working men slept in bunks in the **barracks**.
Rough **shelters** and **tents** were used until buildings could be erected.
Grenville's house was inside the fort.
Livestock was kept in a **pen**.
A **watchtower** allowed guards to see boats approaching.
4
5
Earthwork defenses were made by digging trenches and then using the dirt to fill baskets that would be stacked to make a wall, then covered in more dirt.
A **well** supplied the fort with drinking water in the event that it might be dangerous to leave the walls.
The **laboratory** was used to test the metals in the area. The experiments created toxic smoke, so it had to be kept away from the houses.

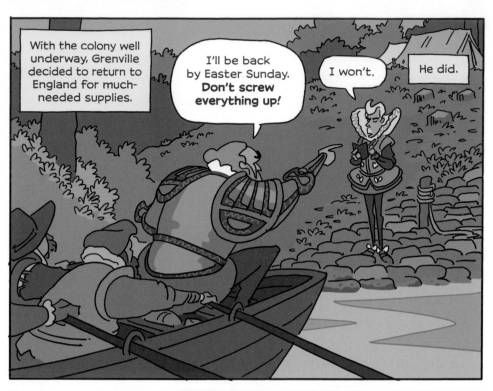

With the colony well underway, Grenville decided to return to England for much-needed supplies.

I'll be back by Easter Sunday. **Don't screw everything up!**

I won't.

He did.

Lane did not treat the Native Americans like **allies** whose willingness to share their harvest kept the colonists alive. He treated them with disdain and took their generosity for granted.

Hey, savages, we're low on corn! Let's shake a leg, huh?

Lane's arrogance did not go unnoticed.

Sachem Wingina, we need to drive these jokers away.

They act like they think they're better than us.

Let's be patient. Maybe they just don't know how to behave in polite society.

Still waiting on that corn, Chief!

The winter months were a hard time to grow, find, or hunt food, so we worked hard the rest of the year to build up a surplus to make sure that we wouldn't run out before spring arrived.

We usually had enough that we could share with our neighbors if they needed some.

But we **didn't** have enough to feed a hundred strangers every day for months on end.

We're HUNGRY!

It was becoming clear that the settlers weren't growing enough crops to support themselves, and that if they continued to eat our food, we would run out before winter was over.

Sachem Wingina, if we don't drive these guys away, we're all going to **starve**!

Let's be patient. Maybe they just don't realize how much our hospitality is costing us.

Still waiting on that corn, Chief!

Wanchese, you're painting a pretty bleak picture.

We had some problems with the settlers, sure, but you're **always** going to have problems with people.

The good outweighed the bad for me. They brought with them written language, neat technology, and a fascinating religion.

I, for one, am **open** to new things, and even when everyone else was souring on our visitors, I was a faithful friend.

I figured that Lane would become less arrogant as he saw how valuable our wisdom of the land and its resources was.

And we'd help the settlers grow their own crops **eventually**. This first year would be a squeaker, but we're tough, and we could get through it together.

Well, I think you're naive, but even **if** we didn't have to worry about the English being rude or eating all of our food...

...or their outbursts of terrible violence and destruction...

...we'd still have something else to worry about. Something **huge**...

...or, rather, something very, very, **very** tiny.

Germs.

The English settlers carried all sorts of germs, diseases, and viruses in their rarely washed, unhealthily fed bodies.

scritch scritch   scritch

People in England had grown up around these germs.

Well, those who **had** grown up.

Only about **four out of ten** English children survived to adulthood, the rest killed mostly by disease and infection.

Those few who **survived** had battle-hardened **immune systems**. They were able to stave off the worst effects of the common European diseases to which they'd already been exposed when they were kids.

But the Native Americans had **never** been exposed to these diseases, and their immune systems had built up no such tolerance.

Nice t'meetcha... ...a... ...a...

...ATC**HOO!**

Gesundheit.

Whenever a new village or tribe would meet the settlers, they would be exposed to these new, killer germs...

...and within a few days, they would start to get sick.

sniff

Death followed the English as they went from village to village, spreading the germs.

Is it just me, or does it seem like these guys almost all die just after meeting us?

I know! It's weird, right?

The settlers never figured out that they were the cause of this near-extinction of Native people. But the Natives did.

We don't know what germs are yet, but it doesn't take a microbiologist to figure out that these guys are killing us with something we can't see.

My guess is that they're shooting us with **invisible bullets**.

Sachem Wingina, **whatever** they're killing us with, they're still **killing us**.

We've got to drive these guys off before we're all worm food!

Let's be patient. Maybe—

Sachem Wingina, I bring news! Your **brother**, Granganimeo, is **dead**.

Yo, Chief! How long you gonna keep us waiting on that corn?

Yeah. We're going to war.

Lane expected the Secotans to be servile to his colony, so he didn't pick up on Wingina's pretty obvious hints.

Hey, Wingina. Whatcha doing?

Putting on my **war decorations**.

I'm adopting a **war name**. From now on you can call me **Pemisipan**.

Cool, cool.

So what's going on with **you** these days?

"Pemisipan" loosely translates to "I've got my eye on you, you arrogant jerk."

Neat. Well, I got stuff to do, Winjee. Keep that corn coming, all right?

Pemisipan had a war plan. He would cut off food supplies to the colony, which would force the settlers to go off in small groups to scavenge what they could. The Secotans would have a better chance battling these small groups than they did fighting the whole well-armed colony.

But, as it turned out, Lane saved him the trouble of having to put his plan into effect.

Hey, Chief, I'm thinking about taking some men exploring up into the wild and dangerous territory of those guys whose village we raided.

...

Yeah. Yeah, you should do that. Go find **Sachem Menatonon**, he's having a council about what to do about you guys.

Menatonon, huh? You think that's a good idea?

Sure. He's **furious** at you for murdering his people, but this would be a **great** chance for you to explain what you're doing here and how you're not responsible for eating all our food and causing all of us to die from some awful and invisible plague.

Sounds like a plan. Thanks, Wingina!

I told you, my name's **Pemisipan** now!

Send word to Menatonon that these knuckleheads are headed his way.

Word reached Menatonon, who was ready and waiting for Lane and his settlers...

...or so he thought.

All right, nobody move! **We're** in charge now!

60

Lane, whose colony depended **entirely** on support from Natives for food and guidance, had succeeded in making **enemies** of all **three** of the Carolina Algonquian nations. Thanks to his actions, the colony was doomed.

Hang on just a minute! We're **not** dependent on these guys.

Grenville will be back with supplies by **Easter**.

We'll be **fine!**

They weren't.

Lane's exploration party took first the sachem and then his son hostage. They traveled far upriver, hoping to find Native gold mines that they could ransack for easy treasure. No such mines existed, but that didn't stop Lane from dreaming.

Everywhere they went, they found empty villages. The people fled as they approached, taking their food with them.

Why would anyone run away? We're so friendly!

The settlers ate what little food they had, then their dogs, then were reduced to boiling leaves for "stew."

By the time they got back to the fort, they were starving.

But hey, it's Easter Sunday! Grenville should be back anytime now!

54 DAYS LATER

Grenville should be back anytime now.

But Grenville wasn't anywhere close.

Shortly after leaving Roanoke, he sighted and captured a large Spanish treasure galleon.

He returned to England with his prize, and the colony was viewed as a **success**.

Not because it was sustainable or thriving (it was neither), but because its investors had made a **profit**, which was the only thing that mattered.

Man alive, I forgot how **hungry** I was back then!

After months of negotiating how the spoils of his prize would be divided, Grenville **finally** set sail for Roanoke...

...but would be **too late** to help anyone there.

I'd spent enough time with the English to see that they were going to be the end of us if we didn't get rid of them.

That's 'cause **you're** a big old pessimistic **grouch**.

I'd hoped that instead of using violence, we could force them to **leave**. I'd talked Pemisipan into cutting off their supply of corn and grains, and I destroyed the fish traps that we had built for them.

They were without food and surrounded by enemies.

Their only allies were Manteo and his family and the Chowanokes, who were only being friendly because the settlers were holding the king's son hostage.

Surely they would figure out that the **only** good course of action would be to **leave**.

Men, we only have **one good course of action**.

We trick King Wingina or Pemisipan or **whatever** he's calling himself into thinking we're **leaving**...

...and when his guard is down, we **attack**!

I don't think they figured out what you **wanted** them to figure out.

Lane and his men, including **me**, attacked and destroyed the Secotan village on Roanoke.

Then, before there was a chance for word to reach Pemisipan, we hurried to the mainland to **ambush** him and the small group with which he traveled.

Pemisipan was **shot**, but was able to escape into the thick forest...

...where he was caught by one of Lane's soldiers, who **killed** him and brought back his **head** as a **trophy**.

How could you **do** this, Manteo?

You helped foreign invaders **murder** your own **sachem**!

I didn't see them as foreign invaders.

I saw them as my **family**.

The English settlers invited me into their community, taught me their language, shared with me their culture, and even baptized me in their religion.

Theirs was a strange and exotic way of life, but I felt a true connection to it.

When I saw the people of my birth starving them out, I felt like it was my **duty** to side with them.

That doesn't mean that I was happy going to war with my own nation.

Well, **speaking** of **war**, England and Spain were now at war for real, even though neither side had officially declared it.

So imagine how nervous Lane was when, fresh from his victory over Pemisipan, he was informed that a **huge** fleet had been sighted sailing in from Spanish waters.

Is it the Spanish?

I can't tell. Telescopes won't be readily available to sailors for another two hundred years!

We're so dead we're so dead we're so dead we're so dead

But they **weren't** so dead.

It wasn't a **Spanish** fleet, but an **English** one.

Led by **Sir Francis Drake**, the fleet had been harassing Spanish ships and attacking its ports in the West Indies.

Drake

Drake, another privateer (on a grander scale than Raleigh), had decided to come up to the Carolina coast to check on his countrymen's colony and to set free the 300 or so Africans and Native Americans he had rescued from Spanish slavery.

Drake thought that their presence in the colony might be helpful, since there would be more men on hand to help with the work.

You guys look like you could use a hand.

I'm sure I can spare **four months'** worth of **food, gunpowder, trade goods,** and other supplies.

⇒gasp⇐

And, since I'm sure you want to further explore this new territory, I'll leave you a beautiful, well-armed small ship **perfect** for these shallow coastal channels, along with two pinnaces and four small boats.

⇒gasp⇐

Wow. Drake was a generous guy!

Thanks, Sir Francis. Your assistance gives us **hope.** We've been short on hope the last few weeks.

We've been short on **everything** the last few weeks.

I didn't think we could take another day of this wild, barren land. It's like **God Himself** wanted to send us limping back to England.

But with a new ship filled with all the supplies we could need, **nothing** will be able to drive us from this place!

Uh, Governor Lane?

I think we've got a **problem.**

Storms off the Carolina coast can be quite fierce.

Sir Francis, we've lost a number of ships, either sunk or blown out to sea.

Including the one we were giving to the colonists, along with the supplies it carried.

That's a shame, but it won't stop a grand English enterprise like ours! I'll give them **another** boat, and—

No.

Excuse me?

No, Sir Francis.

This tragedy confirms my fears: without a natural harbor, any ship at anchor could be squished and sunk by storms.

Between that and the natives wanting to starve us out, a colony here is simply **unsustainable**.

We'll try again farther north, in the Chesapeake Bay, but for now, we'd be awfully grateful if you'd give us all a lift **home**.

I'd be happy to! But gather up your stuff fast...

...another storm is on its way!

The approaching storm really had the waves on the beach crashing. The boats on which the settlers tried to load their stuff capsized or ran aground.

We're going to sink! We've got to throw everything overboard!

In their hurry to get away before the second storm hit, the settlers had to **throw away** almost all of the **maps**, **studies**, **metal experiment results**, and **scientific specimens** that had been painstakingly compiled over the last year.

They also forgot about three colonists who had been sent on an errand to the mainland.

They were never seen again (at least not by their countrymen).

*Well, it's a good thing we left when we did! Another few days and the colony would have **starved**.*

No, it wouldn't have.

Almost immediately after Lane and his colonists left, the first relief ship arrived from England with food and supplies.

Where is everybody?

Shortly after that, Grenville himself returned with another fleet, more supplies and food, and reinforcements.

Where is everybody?

Grenville decided to go back to England with the supplies, but left fifteen men to hold the fort.

It would just **look** bad if we didn't keep the lights on.

One matter that neither the relief ship nor Grenville discussed was the presence of the people whom Drake had rescued from enslavement.

Weeks, maybe only days, after they had been put ashore, they disappeared.

What did they do? Where did they go?

How could three hundred people **vanish** practically overnight?

This is the **first** great mystery of Roanoke, the **first disappearance.**

Did the Africans, Central American Natives, and Florida Natives try to make it home?

Did they join local tribes and assimilate into those cultures?

Or did something more **sinister** befall them? Something that would later befall the next batch of English settlers?

Drake's arrival in England was a big deal. He had sacked Spanish towns in the Americas, bringing back treasure and proving that the Spanish colonies were vulnerable.

Privateering continued to fill the pockets of investors, so even though the Roanoke colony had been a **disaster**, everyone was excited to give it another try, if only to make sure that privateers had an American base from which to strike.

It won't be a disaster **this** time, though!

Yes, we've learned important lessons.

Idle veterans, poor vagabonds, and violent soldiers of fortune make **bad colonists**.

They try to figure out the quickest way to make a bunch of money so that they can get out fast.

Families will make better settlers, because they will actually **settle**.

They'll also be less likely to attack the natives without provocation.

A better relationship with the Indians will be **essential** to the survival of a colony.

Can't argue with that!

And, most important...

...Roanoke Island is a **terrible** place to try to start a colony!

So the English would make **another** attempt to start a colony, this one **nowhere near** the island of Roanoke.

It seemed to Raleigh that putting a military man like Grenville or Lane in charge would again see problems met with military solutions.

That had gone very badly before. Maybe a different sort of man could be the leader.

He appointed **John White**, the artist who had joined the previous voyage to paint the Algonquians, as the new colony's governor.

This is quite a promotion!

England had begun to see a new "middling class" of merchants and tradesmen that was carving a place for itself between the peasants and the aristocracy. It was from this group that White recruited 117 colonists.

Governor White's pregnant daughter, Eleanor White Dare.

Three boats were outfitted to take the colonists.

a flyboat

Lion (the flagship)

a pinnace

And piloting the expedition, again, was the pirate **Simon Fernandes**.

Life at sea was awful for the colonists.

The rocking motion of the boat made people seasick.

Have you ever been seasick? It's **terrible**!

You get dizzy and nauseous and moving at all is miserable. In old galleons like *Lion*, you might be seasick for weeks on end!

In order to not interfere with the sailors doing their work, people were encouraged to stay belowdecks.

Only officers had bunks or hammocks. The colonists were expected to find a corner of the floor, maybe with a blanket.

The air was hot and stale in the living quarters, and with so many people seasick it smelled more and more like **vomit** and **poop** with each passing day.

The water and beer that the colonists drank got increasingly sour and spoiled as the journey progressed.

The food (dried fish, salt-preserved meat, cheese, and hard biscuits) began to rot about halfway through the trip.

It was three weeks before *Lion* finally reached land, a stopover in the Caribbean.

As they passed Rojo Bay, White ordered Fernandes to stop for some much-needed **salt**.

I can't do it! The waters are dangerous. It's too risky.

As they passed Puerto Rico, White ordered Fernandes to stop for pineapple and orange plants so that the colonists could attempt to grow their own.

I'd really rather not.

As they passed Hispaniola, White ordered Fernandes to stop for cattle and other provisions, necessities for the new colony.

No.

White was furious. Fernandes was undermining him at every turn, refusing his orders, and putting the colony in jeopardy.

I **really** don't like our pilot.

Oh, if you think he's bad **now**, wait until we get to the next page.

After nearly crashing the ship on more than one occasion, Fernandes finally guided *Lion* up to Roanoke.

I'd bet those fifteen guys Grenville left here will be glad to see some friendly faces.

Why don't we stop here for a day or two and let all of the colonists stretch their legs before we continue north to the Chesapeake Bay?

Fernandes, that's the first thing you've said this whole trip that doesn't sound shady.

Maybe you're okay after all.

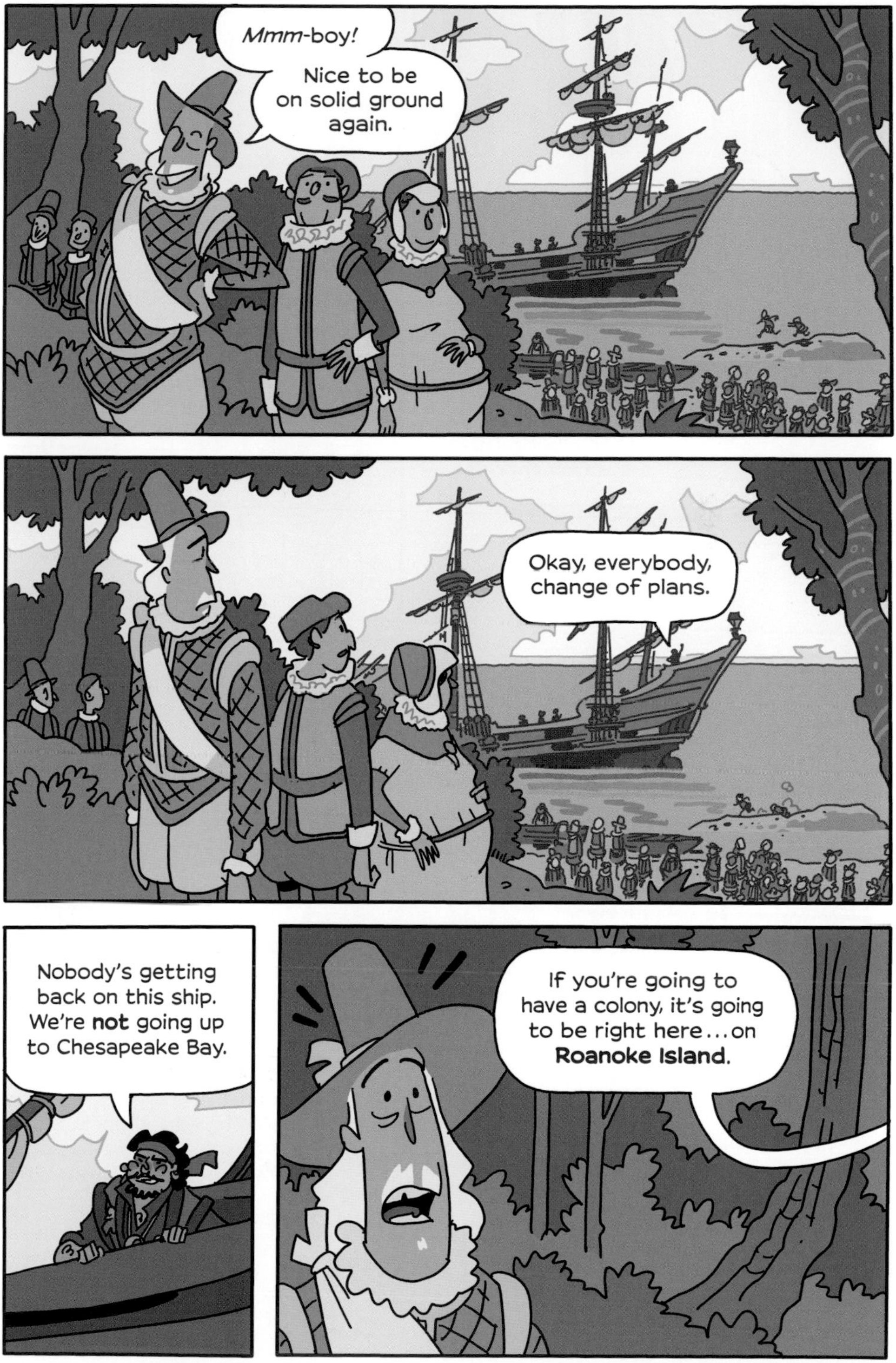
Mmm-boy!
Nice to be on solid ground again.
Okay, everybody, change of plans.
Nobody's getting back on this ship. We're **not** going up to Chesapeake Bay.
If you're going to have a colony, it's going to be right here...on **Roanoke Island**.

Simon Fernandes's unexpected decision to leave the colonists on Roanoke has baffled historians for centuries. It's the **second** great mystery of the Roanoke Colony!

So what motivated him to do it? There are a few theories.

Theory #1: Simon Fernandes was a secret agent for the Spanish Empire!

John White was convinced that Fernandes was a secret Catholic and that he was still in league with his old Spanish masters.

Ha, ha!

Theory #2: Simon Fernandes was a secret agent for the British Empire!

Fernandes had been rescued from execution by Francis Walsingham, the queen's spymaster. Walsingham may have seen value in Fernandes beyond just his ability as a pilot.

You answer to **me** now.

Theory #3: Simon Fernandes was impatient to go on grand and bloody pirate adventures!

Fernandes would get a share of the colony's profits...if there **were** any.

His ship was well armed and well manned, and if he could find Spanish ships carrying their treasure across the ocean then he would be in the perfect position to attack them!

I **am** a pirate. It's **hard** to say no to **treasure**.

But the treasure galleons made their last runs in the summer, before the weather changed. Summer was almost over!

If we take the time to go all the way up to Chesapeake, we'll miss whatever chance we have to catch them!

This suspicion was based more on English prejudices of the time than it was on evidence.

> Hear me out, guys... his last name is **Fernandes**. That **sounds** pretty Spanishy. He's **got** to be a spy!

This theory is probably the least likely, because Fernandes had been preying on Spanish shipping for years. But it wouldn't be the first time that someone was turned into a double agent for the country they had been fighting against. Spain was very wealthy, and could have offered Fernandes a **lot** to play a long and careful game of sabotage and deceit.

> I **am** a pirate. It's **hard** to say no to **treasure**.

Walsingham wanted to hurt the Spanish in any way he could. He liked the **idea** of a privateering base in the Americas, but he might have felt that his **influence** over the queen was **threatened** by Walter Raleigh.

> Excuse me, your majesty...

> Not now, Walsingham. We're busy flirting!

The failure of Raleigh's colony might knock the hot boy out of the queen's favor, putting Walsingham back on top.

> Do whatever you have to, and make sure that this venture never has a chance.

Fernandes, eager for a chance to get rich quick, may have looked for any excuse to speed up the colonists' journey, which would explain why he had refused to stop for provisions...

...and why he left them on Roanoke, much closer than the Chesapeake Bay.

> If you lived **here**, you'd already be home!

> **All** of these theories are **possible**. But there's still one more explanation...

Theory #4: Simon Fernandes wasn't treacherous at all!

Seriously, why does everyone always think the worst of me?

White was an artist, **not** a seaman, an engineer, a military man, or a diplomat.

My paintings are **really** good, though.

His requests of Fernandes throughout the voyage may have been unsafe or unreasonable, and Fernandes was experienced enough to see the danger and avoid it.

Ooh, let's stop for pineapples!

There's a Spanish fort with giant cannons **right next to** the pineapple stand, buddy.

Fernandes knew that even though the English settlers had alienated the Carolina Algonquians with their bad behavior, the Algonquians were still ambivalent about attacking the settlers outright.

The Chesapeake Natives, however, had slaughtered a large group of Spanish missionaries and attacked the first English expedition. They were unified, organized, and ready for war with anyone caught invading.

We **need** to make our way up to the Chesapeake Bay for our new colony!

Surviving will be as easy as pie up **there**!

Oh, you simple, simple man.

You're gonna be staying here on **Roanoke**.

Maybe Fernandes refused to carry White farther for the colonists' own safety.

Knowing they had no choice but to stay on Roanoke, White and the others made their way to the fort. Or, rather, what was **left** of it.

The **earthworks** have all been torn down and the ground flattened. It's not a fort at all anymore.

At least the **buildings** are all still standing.

This one has **deer** living in it!

I thought that Grenville left fifteen men here. Where are they?

I found one of them!

That doesn't seem like a good sign.

The colonists got to work doing the mild repairs needed on the existing buildings...

...and erecting new cottages so that each family would have its own little house.

My baby's going to arrive soon, so we're making **my** family's house first!

Eleanor White Dare

The settlers had left England divided between two ships, and they had been separated early on. The second ship finally arrived at Roanoke as the settlers got up the last of their new cottages.

This is great! Everybody's here, and our houses are all up. Things couldn't be going more smoothly.

Let's get working on our **food**. You guys, start building fishing weirs like the Indians taught us.

You guys get to hunting some deer.

You guys start tilling the earth so that we can plant crops.

The beach is full of crabs. Why don't I go get a bunch for everyone's dinner?

When colonist George Howe left for his crab hunt, it would be the last time any of the colonists would see him alive.

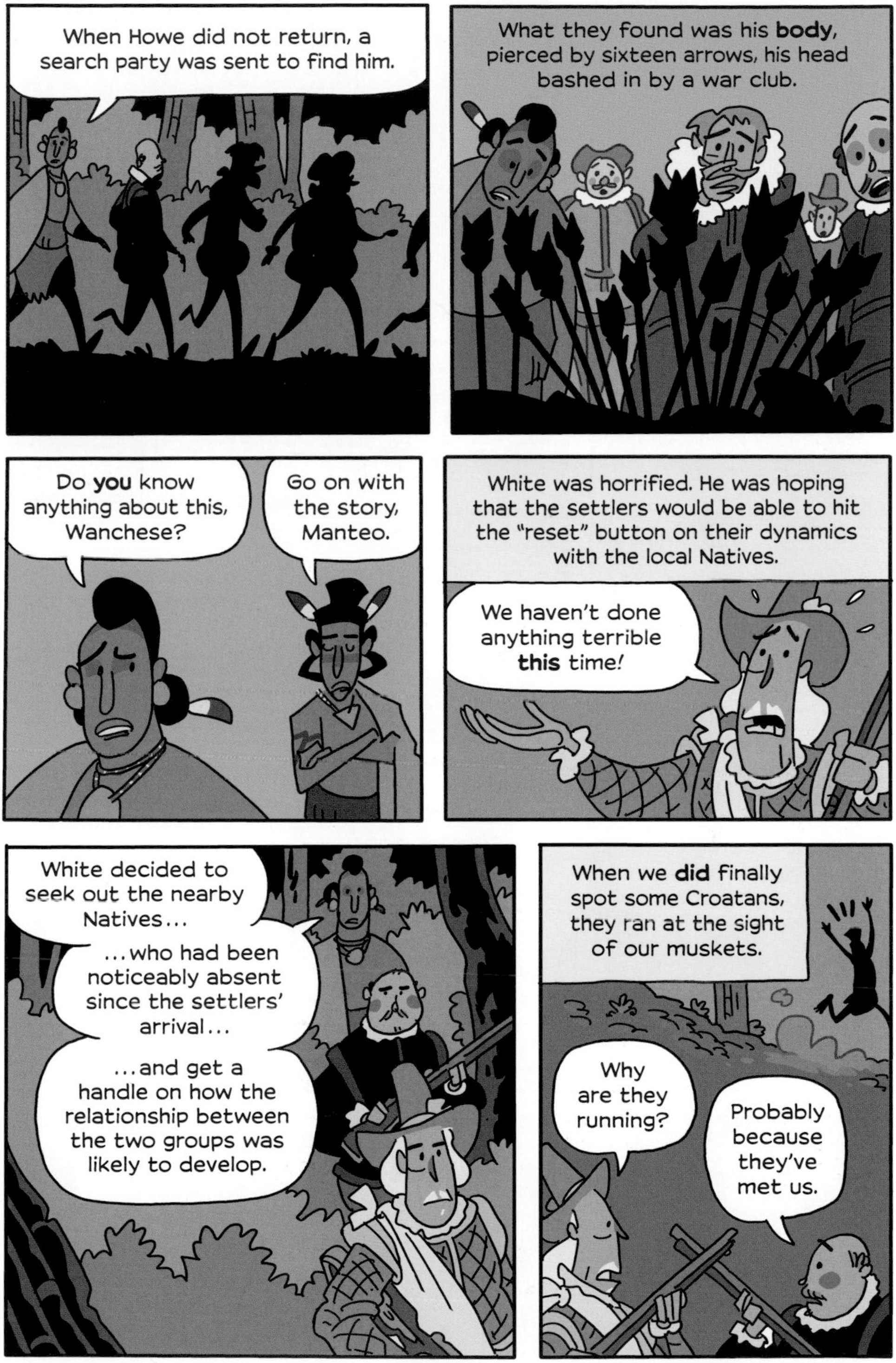
When Howe did not return, a search party was sent to find him.
What they found was his **body**, pierced by sixteen arrows, his head bashed in by a war club.
Do **you** know anything about this, Wanchese?
Go on with the story, Manteo.
White was horrified. He was hoping that the settlers would be able to hit the "reset" button on their dynamics with the local Natives.
We haven't done anything terrible **this** time!
White decided to seek out the nearby Natives...
...who had been noticeably absent since the settlers' arrival...
...and get a handle on how the relationship between the two groups was likely to develop.
When we **did** finally spot some Croatans, they ran at the sight of our muskets.
Why are they running?
Probably because they've met us.

Hey, guys, wait up!

It's me, Manteo!

Manteo?

Hey, buddy!

These settlers haven't murdered you yet!

We kind of figured you'd been murdered.

No, **these** are my people, **too**! They wouldn't murder **me**.

Maybe not on purpose. They don't always seem like they're capable of making rational decisions.

Hey, Manteo, we're fine with your settler friends being on the island again, but we've got to talk about **food**.

Last time they were here, we shared more than we could spare. But at least we had food **to** share.

What do you mean?

We're low on food stores. **Dangerously** low. We don't have enough for **ourselves**, much less anyone else.

If we can't figure out a way to get our hands on some corn, we're toast!

Don't worry, the English are making smart food decisions this time around.

Yeah, we're not looking for **food**. We're just looking for **revenge!**

Hang on, we're looking for **what**?

Revenge, silly! Somebody killed our man George Howe, and we're going to make them pay for it.

I thought we were trying to turn over a new leaf, stop the whole cycle of violence.

Well we are, sure, but that doesn't mean we're not going to destroy the village of whoever had the audacity to confront us! Manteo, sometimes you crack me up.

So... who killed Howe?

It was a war party of **Secotans**, still angry about the murder of Sachem Pemisipan...

...they were led by **Wanchese**.

Wanchese! Say it ain't **so**, old friend!

Wanchese, you're scaring me.

The English had proven that they were **dangerous neighbors**.

They had no qualms about taking our food, destroying our homes, and even killing us.

The diseases that they carried wiped out huge portions of our population.

Even the kindest and most generous of them saw us as inferior, and to them "living in harmony" would simply mean that we would have to adopt **their** religion, customs, and way of life.

I could see clearly that if they were to stay in America, it would be the end of our way of life, and perhaps the end of our very **existence**.

I had no choice but to rise up against those who would **destroy** us.

The response of your governor was all the proof I needed that I was right to take my stand.

Very well. I don't **want** to, but we've got no choice...

...we've got to **attack** the Secotans and **wipe them out**!

See?

Okay, but we **Croatans** are your **allies**, right?

You guys have a terrible track record with telling us apart. How about you give us some kind of **symbol** that we can wear to **show** that we're allies?

A badge or a hat or **something**.

I feel like it would be a good idea for us to have a way to identify ourselves on sight so that you don't kill **us** by mistake.

Ha! Oh, my Croatan friend, you give us too little credit. There's **no way** we'd mistake you for enemies and kill you by accident!

But just a few days later...

This is why I said we needed a badge!

Oops.

White and the others attacked my Croatan brothers and sisters?

Why?!

What happened?!

Word got out about White's intention to attack Wanchese's Secotan village.

Those Secotans won't know what hit 'em!

The Secotans evacuated...

...and the starving Croatans, hearing that the Secotans had abandoned their village, went to go scavenge whatever food from it they could.

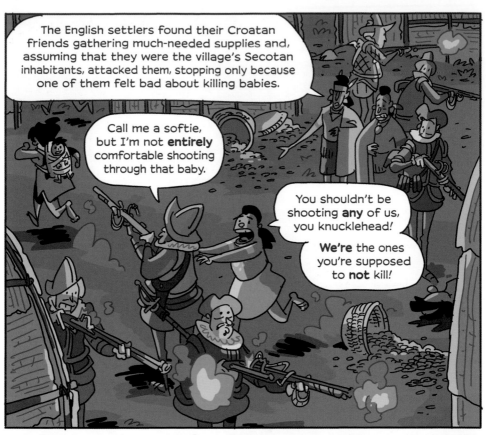

The English settlers found their Croatan friends gathering much-needed supplies and, assuming that they were the village's Secotan inhabitants, attacked them, stopping only because one of them felt bad about killing babies.

Call me a softie, but I'm not **entirely** comfortable shooting through that baby.

You shouldn't be shooting **any** of us, you knucklehead!

We're the ones you're supposed to **not** kill!

White felt just terrible about his mistake, and the consequences it was sure to have in their future relations with the Natives.

We're still **friends**, right?

Um, yeeeaah.

Sure.

But we, uh, we've got a few errands to run, so, uh, we're gonna go.

Bye!

We're never going to see them again, are we?

Things weren't looking good.

We still had the food we'd brought from England, and it would last us for a few months...

...but without help from the local tribes, we'd have to be careful rationing it.

We arrived after the growing season, so our crops would be meager at best.

And the settlers knew that if they went off in small, unprotected groups, I would probably attack them with my soldiers.

This meant that they couldn't fish, and they **certainly** couldn't go out hunting for meat.

Any group large enough to be safe against me would scare off whatever scarce game they were hoping to hunt.

We needed more supplies from England. **And** we needed **reinforcements**.

But we needed them soon. How could we make **sure** that they would arrive?

We needed someone to return to England for us to convince Sir Walter Raleigh that it was essential to send this help right away. And we knew **exactly** who that "someone" should **be**.

You want me to **what**?!

You're the best person for the job, Governor!

Raleigh listens to you!

There isn't anyone else here with your clout. If **you** don't go, **we** might end up low on everyone's list of priorities.

Please, Governor! We beg you!

White was torn. He wanted to help the colony...

...especially his brand-new **granddaughter**, Virginia Dare, the first English person born in America...

...but he was worried that his reputation would be ruined if he abandoned his duties as governor of the colony just weeks after arriving.

Also, I'm worried about leaving my **stuff**!

We'll take real good care of your stuff, Governor.

In fact, we'll all take a **solemn oath** to take care of your stuff.

They weren't kidding. All of the colonists signed a document promising to take care of White's stuff if he would return to England on their behalf.

It might be the very first English contract drawn up in America!

Of course, it's entirely possible that the colonists just wanted to get White out of their hair.

With no leadership experience, his decision-making and inability to control Fernandes might have made the colonists worry for their fate if left in his hands.

Remember when he wanted to get pineapples from the Spanish fort?

Jeez, don't remind me.

Whether they thought he could really help or whether they were just trying to get rid of him, the colonists finally succeeded in convincing White to leave.

Oh! How will I find you if you need to move to another location?

We'll carve the **name** of our destination in a **tree**!

And if we're **attacked** or forced to leave, we'll carve a **cross** over it.

Have a good trip! Bring me back something English!

White's journey did **not** go smoothly.

The capstan, which hauls up the anchor, broke, spinning its heavy levers around and injuring a lot of the sailors.

The food either spoiled or ran out...

...and just as they reached the coast of Ireland a fierce storm blew them halfway back across the Atlantic Ocean.

No! We're so close!

It was a long voyage, but at least White would be able to get a relief fleet organized immediately!

Sir Walter, I need you to organize a relief fleet immediately!

Oh. Then I've got some bad news.

Spain was readying its Armada (a huge battle fleet) to attack and conquer England.

England, vastly outgunned and outnumbered, required every battle-ready boat to be on hand for when the attack finally came.

No large ships would be allowed to leave England for America.

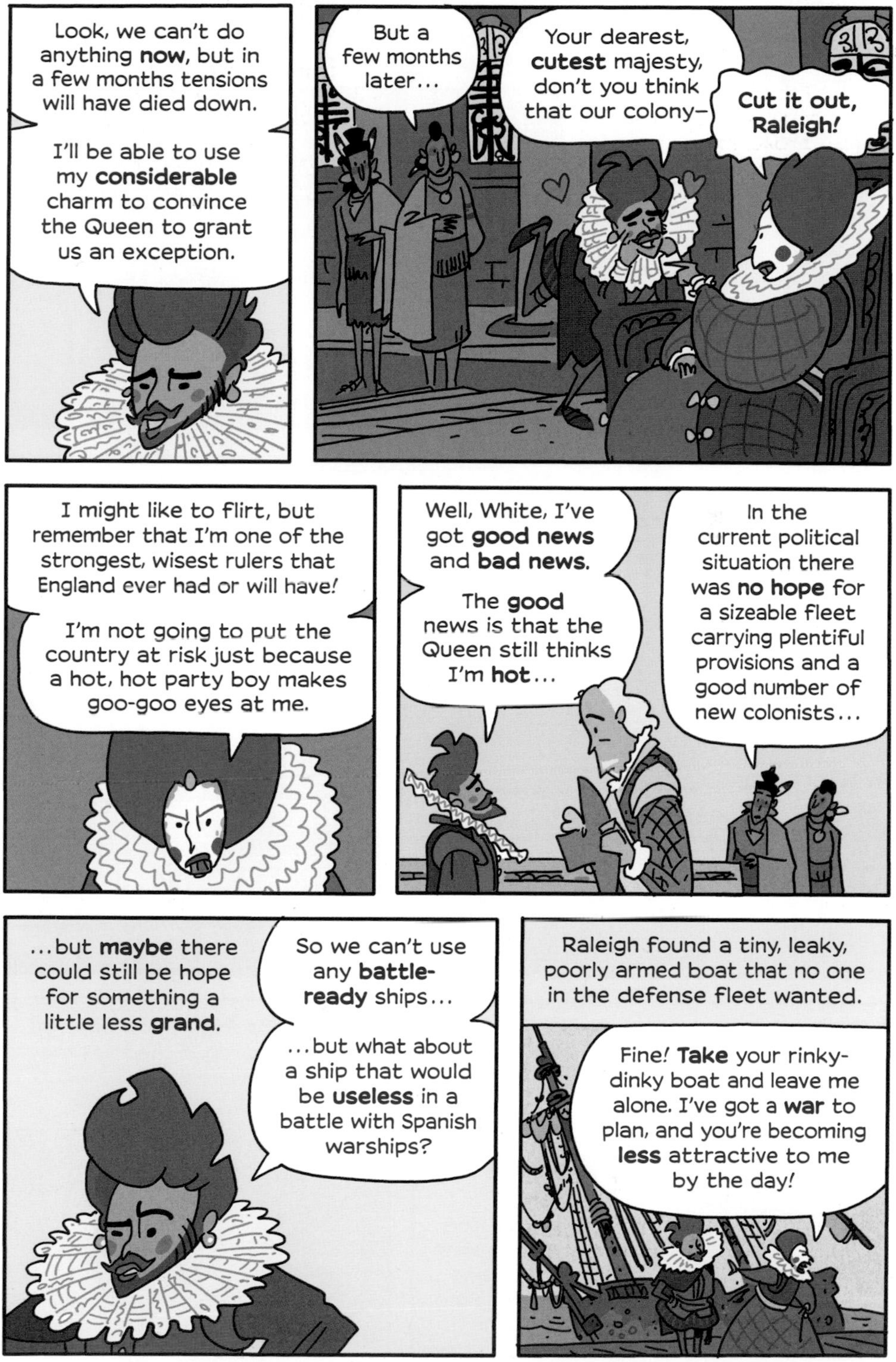

Look, we can't do anything **now**, but in a few months tensions will have died down.
I'll be able to use my **considerable** charm to convince the Queen to grant us an exception.
But a few months later...
Your dearest, **cutest** majesty, don't you think that our colony–
Cut it out, Raleigh!
I might like to flirt, but remember that I'm one of the strongest, wisest rulers that England ever had or will have!
I'm not going to put the country at risk just because a hot, hot party boy makes goo-goo eyes at me.
Well, White, I've got **good news** and **bad news**.
The **good** news is that the Queen still thinks I'm **hot**...
In the current political situation there was **no hope** for a sizeable fleet carrying plentiful provisions and a good number of new colonists...
...but **maybe** there could still be hope for something a little less **grand**.
So we can't use any **battle-ready** ships...
...but what about a ship that would be **useless** in a battle with Spanish warships?
Raleigh found a tiny, leaky, poorly armed boat that no one in the defense fleet wanted.
Fine! **Take** your rinky-dinky boat and leave me alone. I've got a **war** to plan, and you're becoming **less** attractive to me by the day!

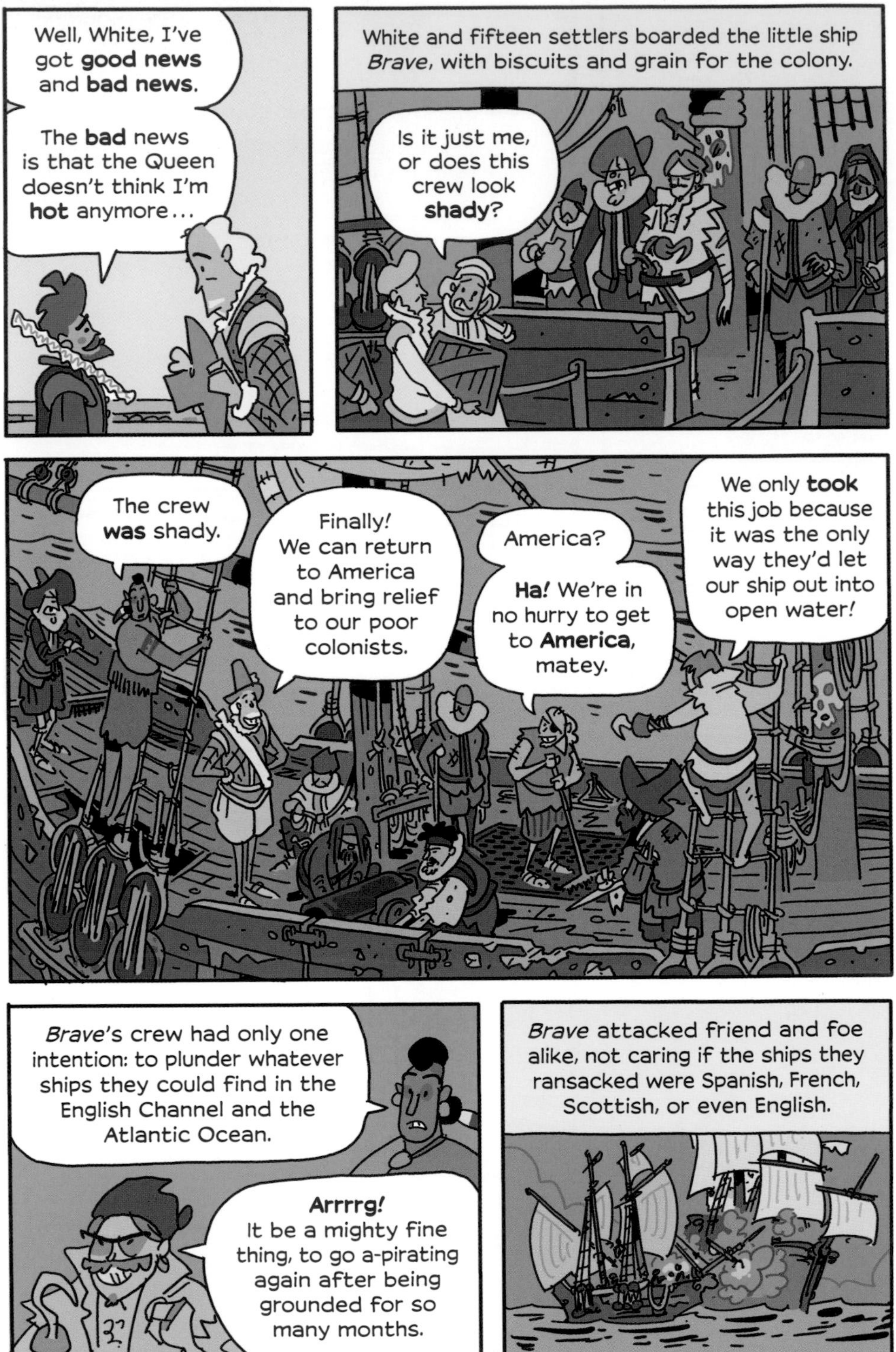
Well, White, I've got **good news** and **bad news**.
The **bad** news is that the Queen doesn't think I'm **hot** anymore...
White and fifteen settlers boarded the little ship *Brave*, with biscuits and grain for the colony.
Is it just me, or does this crew look **shady**?
The crew **was** shady.
Finally! We can return to America and bring relief to our poor colonists.
America?
Ha! We're in no hurry to get to **America**, matey.
We only **took** this job because it was the only way they'd let our ship out into open water!
Brave's crew had only one intention: to plunder whatever ships they could find in the English Channel and the Atlantic Ocean.
Arrrrg! It be a mighty fine thing, to go a-pirating again after being grounded for so many months.
Brave attacked friend and foe alike, not caring if the ships they ransacked were Spanish, French, Scottish, or even English.

Their short and bloody cruise was finally stopped by a French ship, whose attack overwhelmed the undisciplined pirates.

Many in the pirate crew were killed, and three of the new colonists were badly injured.

John White was hurt, too... three times!

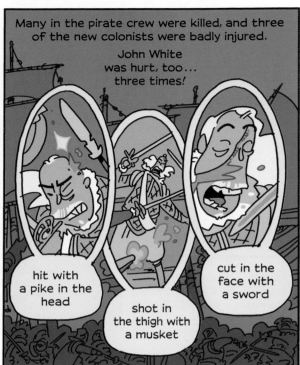

hit with a pike in the head

shot in the thigh with a musket

cut in the face with a sword

The Frenchmen spared the English crew once they had surrendered, **but** they carried off the few provisions that White had been able to secure for the colony.

With the ship in tatters, its crew nearly wiped out, its supplies gone, and its captain and mate close to death, White had no choice but to limp back to England, his mission unfinished.

He would not leave again that spring, or even that year.

White would not return to the colonists a couple of months after he left, like they'd hoped.

It would take **three long years** before he set foot on the island again.

A lot happened between White's disastrous trip and his next chance to return to Roanoke.

The Spanish finally attacked, sending 130 giant warships to invade England.

Queen Elizabeth and her commanders had only 50 smaller ships, but were able to soundly defeat the Spanish.

Raleigh was rewarded with a large estate in Ireland, which took most of his attention.

Raleigh's colony in Ireland left him few resources to devote to Roanoke.

I'm really busy trying to conquer the Irish, White. Maybe come back **next** year.

White was desperate. He pleaded and searched and plotted and begged but couldn't find anyone who would finance a relief expedition.

He felt terrible. He had **promised** his friends and family that he would bring them help, and he had **failed**.

Finally, in 1590, he heard about a large privateering fleet that was heading to the West Indies to attack Spanish treasure ships.

White convinced the pirates to let him come along.

You can come, but **no** colonists and **no** supplies!

We'll need all of that room for **treasure**.

The Roanoke Colony had been forgotten and abandoned by its organizers, and even though White had nothing to offer them, he wanted them to know that **he** hadn't forgotten them, too.

White found himself waiting a long time. The privateers spent **weeks** attacking Spanish ships in American waters.

They were also delayed when their Spanish navigator **escaped** and fled to Spanish authorities.

Remember how the English had few pilots or navigators of their own?

They would often kidnap Spanish or Portuguese ones and force them into service.

Finally, with plenty of loot and treasure in their holds, the privateer ships headed north for Roanoke.

But weather was bad, and when they tried to land nearby the swelling sea swamped some of the boats.

Despite attempts to save them, one of the ships' captains, its mate, and five other seamen were drowned.

The crew wanted to leave. They missed their homes and had piles of treasure just waiting to be divided up.

Why risk their lives further just to check on some colonists when they were so close to the finish line?

The remaining captain, now a friend of White's, convinced them to stay one more day, to see to the fate of their countrymen.

They waited until the morning. White's hopes and fears battled as they anticipated making landfall.

The seas were just as dangerous as they had been the day before. The small boats carrying White and the landing party barely made it to shore.

No one came out to greet the privateers as they made their way toward the settlement.

White was startled when the colony came into view. It wasn't simply the cluster of small buildings that had been there when he left. It was now entirely surrounded by a defensive **palisade**.

What were they protecting themselves **against**?

As the approaching storm began to fill the sky with thunder, White and his party entered the settlement...

This is **really** spooky.

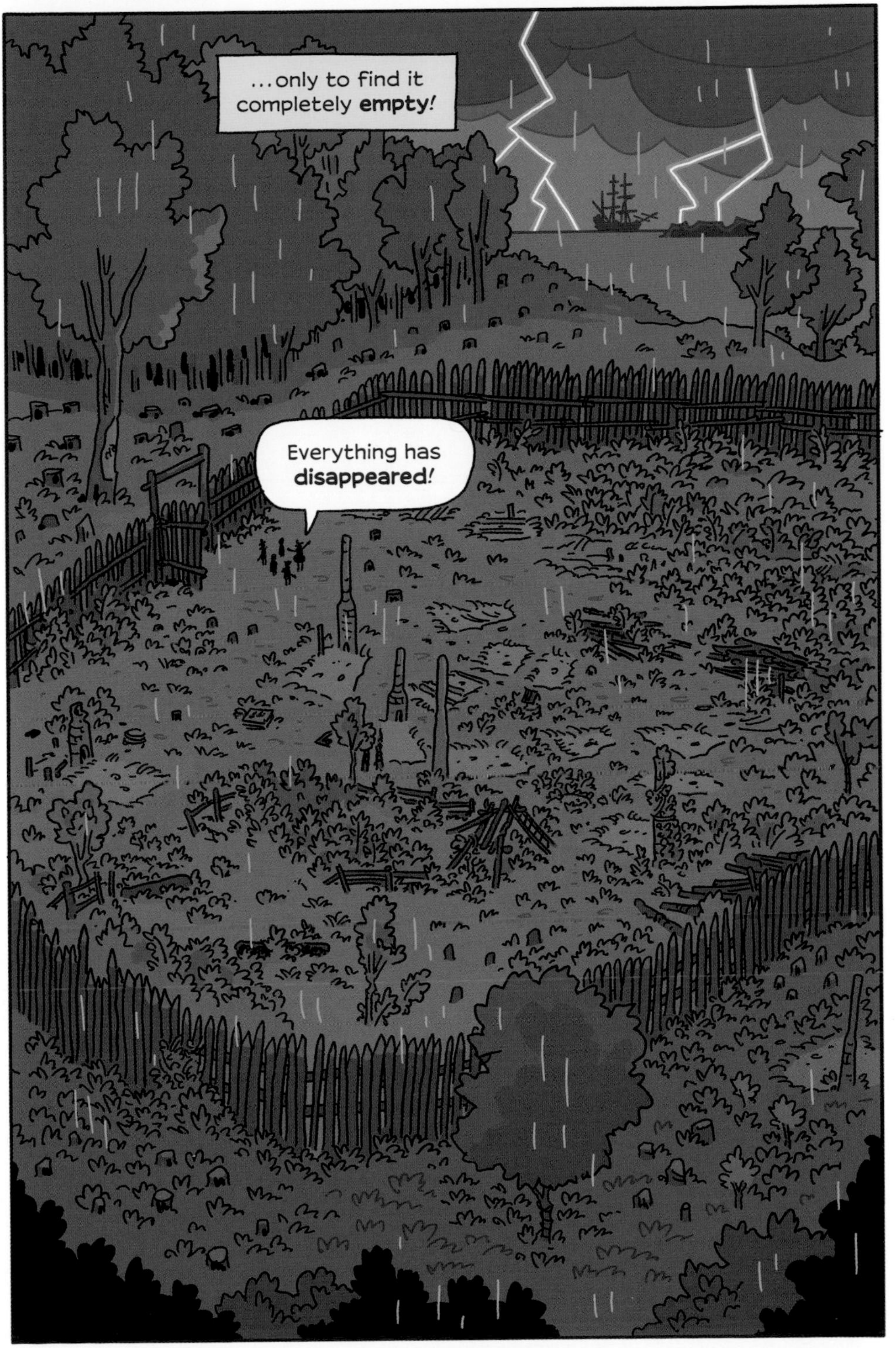
...only to find it completely **empty**!
Everything has **disappeared**!

Where is everyone?

Where are the buildings?

Governor! Over here!

Look... carved into the tree!

CROATOAN

"Cro-a-to-an."

What does it mean?

It's a magic **spell**!

A spell that transported everyone here straight to the devil's domain!

Woe be to us! Merely by casting our eyes on such witchery we might find ourselves likewise fated!

Guys, guys!

"Croatoan" **isn't** some sinister **magic word**.

It's the name of a nearby island. Our friend Manteo is from there.

The colonists said that if they left they would carve the name of their destination in a tree.

They're on **Croatoan**!

Why would they go **there**?

That's a **mystery**, but it won't remain one for long. We'll make our way to Croatoan and ask them!

But White and the privateers **didn't** go to Croatoan.

The storm blew them out to sea.

They decided to refit in the West Indies and try again . . .

. . . only to again find themselves hit by a storm.

To White's dismay, the crew insisted that they return to England without making another attempt to reach Croatoan.

It would be almost **twenty years** before another English soul would set out to find the colonists.

 But by then, they were long gone, **never** to be seen by English eyes **again**.

 **What happened to the colonists?**

 It's America's greatest unsolved mystery, but now **you** have all the **facts**.

No one living knows for certain, but for more than **four hundred years** people have been proposing **theories**.

ROANOKE: WHAT HAPPENED?

WHERE ARE THE COLONIST

ROANOKE MYSTERY

WHERE'S ROANOKE

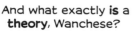 And what exactly **is** a **theory**, Wanchese?

Well, Manteo, in this case it means an **explanation** for something that can't be proved **or** disproved because there isn't enough evidence.

It's an **educated guess** about what happened based on what we **know**.

 **Some** of these theories are quite **plausible**.

Others are a little more... **imaginative**.

We now come to the part of the book that you've been waiting for...

A WHOLE BUNCH OF THEORIES about THE ROANOKE DISAPPEARANCE

Proceed with caution: some of these theories may be hazardous to your **sanity!**

THEORY: CAPTURED (OR KILLED!) BY THE SPANISH

The Spanish recognized the danger that an English settlement in the New World presented. It would be just what the English intended it to be: a base from which they could strike out against Spanish treasure galleons.

Would the Spanish try to **find** this dangerous settlement? They would... and they **did**!

Captain Vicente González led an expedition of soldiers from Spanish Florida to Virginia. Their mission? **Find** the English and **destroy** them!

The Spanish searched the Chesapeake Bay and the rivers that fed into it, but found no trace of the English.

Finding nothing, they gave up, and headed back to Florida, but heavy winds made them pull behind some small barrier islands for shelter. Barrier islands sitting just off the **North Carolina coast**.

The soldiers saw barrels and other signs of English presence.

They had landed on **Roanoke Island**!

The soldiers readied their weapons and prepared to attack the settlers...

...but there weren't any.

The island was **empty**.

Captain González had arrived on Roanoke almost a full year after White departed for England, and by this time, the colonists weren't on the island anymore.

There were no English pirates to capture or kill, but González had found their nest...

...and he reported its location to the Spanish authorities.

Those authorities might have used that location as a starting point from which to search for any English colonists still nearby.

Thanks to the hints left behind by the Roanoke settlers, the Spanish would've known just where to look...

...and could have killed the colonists there or forced them to spend the rest of their days working the mines in Central America or the plantations in Florida and Cuba.

THEORY: ASSIMILATED INTO THE ALGONQUIAN NATIONS

Roanoke Island had little game to hunt and poor soil for crops. The settlers couldn't survive for very long without new supplies arriving.

While a handful may have gone to Croatoan with Manteo so that they would be within sight of any ships approaching Roanoke, most would have traveled inland, since the Croatans had no food to share.

Wanchese and his warriors would **not** have made them welcome in Secotan villages, so they would have gone to the Chowanokes and the nearby Tuscaroras.

When settlers came to America twenty years later, there were reports of English people living in four different towns among the Tuscaroras and the Chowanokes.

Some of these villages had stone houses, built in the English fashion, and there were crosses and English letters carved into trees.

PAS

ACB

Generations later, a surveyor from Charleston met Natives who knew how to read and write English, the old language of their great-grandparents.

NICE WIG, STRANGER

With no English ships coming to their rescue, the colonists would have settled into life with their Algonquian neighbors.

They would have, by necessity, adopted Algonquian ways of life, and their children would have grown up as Algonquians themselves.

THEORY: KILLED BY THE NATIVES ON WHOSE LAND THEY'D SETTLED

When White left, he knew that he was leaving the colonists in hostile territory. They had made enemies of nearly all of their neighbors.

Wanchese was ready to bring war to the settlers, and may have attacked the colony with a large band of soldiers.

The settlers fought them off, but knew that they were in trouble. They would have built a palisade for better defense...the palisade that White found upon his return.

The palisade may have kept them alive during a later attack, but if they were trapped inside they would eventually have run out of food.

Perhaps Wanchese would have starved them out, storming the fort when they became too weak to defend it...

Or, if he withdrew, the settlers may have taken the opportunity to retreat from their indefensible position, packing up their buildings and belongings and heading to Croatoan.

Though that might have been Wanchese's plan all along. He and his soldiers could have **ambushed** the colonists as they made their way to Croatoan, wiping them out as they were burdened with their belongings, unable to mount a defense.

THEORY: MAGICALLY TRANSFORMED INTO WHITE DEER

This is a story that assumes that the colonists went to live among other Native villages.

Little Virginia Dare, the first English child born in America, grew into a wise and beautiful young woman, and fell in love with Okisko of the Weapemeocs.

But a sorceror named Chico desired Virginia for his own.

Virginia was having none of it; she only had eyes for Okisko.

Enraged that Virginia would choose another, Chico used his magic to transform her into a white deer.

Okisko, heartbroken when he learned of Virginia's fate, fashioned a magic arrowhead that would remove the spell and change her back into a human being.

But Wanchese, not knowing that this deer was, in fact, a magic creature, set out to hunt it.

The two hunters found Virginia at the same time, and loosed their arrows at her.

Virginia was transformed by Okisko's arrow, but Wanchese's arrow ended her life. She died in Okisko's arms.

My bad.

Her blood fell to the ground, and from that spot grew the first scuppernong grapes from which North Carolina wine would be made.

THEORY: THE COLONISTS BECAME WENDIGOAG

In Algonquian legend, a wendigo is a terrible and evil creature that used to be a person.

A person can become a wendigo by being greedy, dying with injustice never atoned for on their head, overeating when others are starving, or being a cannibal.

What's a cannibal?

A person who **eats** another person.

Yuck!

Perhaps the settlers were punished for having the audacity to claim the land of others as their own...

Perhaps, starving in the winter, they resorted to eating their own dead...

Whatever their crime, the settlers were transformed into ravenous monsters.

Unable to fill their bellies, unable to die except at the hands of a hero who would save others from their hunger, the colonists would roam the eastern United States for centuries to come...

...becoming the basis for stories about Bigfoot, the Jersey Devil, the Florida Swamp Ape, and other cryptid creatures.

THEORY: ABDUCTED BY ALIENS

In 1561, there was a terrible battle over Germany between three large battleships. Two alien races duked it out in the sky for more than an hour, launching hundreds of fighters, many of which crashed into the sea and the German countryside.

Though most of the crashed fighters were destroyed and the battleships long gone, the aliens that **did** survive wanted to get home. Some sent out distress signals and were rescued on August 7, 1566, when ships appeared over Switzerland to retrieve their fallen comrades.

But some of these ships, falling high from the atmosphere, landed too far away to be spotted by rescue craft. One such fighter may have found itself stranded in the **Carolina wilderness**.

Its communication systems damaged beyond repair and far from any technology that they could use, the aliens were forced to slowly and painstakingly repair their ship. If they were using **biotechnology**, it would have taken **years** to grow enough components to make all of the repairs necessary for interstellar travel.

The aliens probably had some violent encounters early on with the nearby Natives, and would have kept their distance.

But when they spotted the Roanoke settlers with their metal armor and metal tools, the aliens would have considered them too valuable to not use in their endeavors.

Shortly after White left, the aliens captured the colonists, taking their tools to be melted down for parts and forcing them to labor on repairing the spacecraft.

At the end of 1608, the spacecraft was repaired enough to attempt to break the atmosphere. The settlers were either forced to come along, or, eager to see the wider universe, volunteered.

The ship failed to break orbit, however, and the aliens were forced to land in Korea. It would take almost another year before the ship was ready for flight again.

On September 26, 1609, the ship made another attempt, this one successful.

The aliens, and the Lost Colonists, disappeared into the stars.

Did the humans become part of some alien zoo?

Or did they carve out new lives for themselves on alien planets as explorers, mercenaries, artists, or space pirates?

Perhaps one day, should aliens come to visit Earth again, we will find the descendants of the Lost Colony among them!

THEORY: TRANSPORTED TO ANOTHER PLANE OF EXISTENCE

The colonists—hungry, cramped, under threat of attack, and forgotten by their home country—would probably have fought among themselves often.
One of the settlers couldn't take it anymore. They were pushed too far, and decided to get their revenge.
Perhaps this settler had learned witchcraft back in England.
Maybe they conjured up a demon in the wilderness who taught them evil magic.
One way or another, they learned a terrible spell that would cause everyone in the colony to vanish, transported to another dimension, time, or even to hell itself.
The word "Croatoan," carved into the tree, was **not**, in fact, the name of their destination, but the **magic word** that activated the spell.
CROAT
In an instant, each and every colonist disappeared, never to be seen again.

THEORY: SAVED BY THE AFRICANS THAT DRAKE RESCUED

The colonists, starving and under threat of attack from Wanchese and his soldiers, went with Manteo to Croatoan Island, but the starving Croatans turned them away.

Wandering the wilderness, scavenging to survive, they encountered some of the men whom Drake had rescued from slavery and released into Carolina two years earlier.

These men were part of larger settlements, far inland to avoid recapture by the Spanish, that traded and intermarried with the Pamlicos and other people to the south, on a trade route that may have stretched as far south as north Florida.

The settlers, initially unwelcome among the Indians whose hospitality they had so abused, were received by the displaced Africans, and all were slowly accepted by the neighboring Native communities into which they eventually assimilated.

So which one do **you** think happened?

To answer **that**, we need to look to the first person who ever set out to unravel the Roanoke mystery. America's **first** **detective**...

...Captain **John Smith**.

The guy from the Pocahontas story?

That's him!

John Smith was a tough-as-nails veteran soldier. He was part of the **Jamestown Colony**, the first **permanent** English settlement in America. It began **twenty years** after the settlement at Roanoke.

Smith, on a mission to find food for the colony, was captured by the local Powhatan Indians in a frozen swamp and was taken to their sachem, Wahunsenacah.

There he was famously rescued from execution by eleven-year-old Princess Pocahontas.

Safe from harm, Smith enjoyed daily conversations with Wahunsenacah. One day, the sachem said something startling...

You dress like those guys who live down in Ocahonan.

Smith didn't know where Ocahonan was, but he **did** know the story of the lost Roanoke Colony.

If there were people wearing English clothes along the Carolina coast, they **must** be the missing colonists!

When he returned to Jamestown, Smith sent a search party to go south to find the lost colonists. The party was turned back by native guards, but they were able to confirm that the colonists were in Ocahonan. In fact, there were **four** villages in which English colonists still lived, spread throughout Chowanoke and Tuscarora territory!

Political infighting at the Jamestown Settlement and increasing conflict with the Powhatans kept Smith too busy to mount another search party, and it was a year before he tried again to find the missing colonists. In early 1609, he sent his two best men to find and bring back the colonists.

The men searched and investigated and came back to Smith with **bad news.**

Smith recorded their findings... ...and closed the case.

'Twas nothing we could learn but they were **DEAD**

"Dead"?! But Wahunsenacah said they were **alive!** What happened?

That question brings us to our **final theory...**

THEORY: THE SEARCH FOR THE LOST COLONISTS LED TO THEIR DEATHS

The colonists likely **did** go to live with different tribes in order to survive that first winter, assimilating into the towns and villages that welcomed them.

For nearly **twenty years**, they lived peacefully in their new communities.

But when the Jamestown settlers arrived, it made them **dangerous** to mighty Wahunsenacah.

Blocked in the north by the Iroquois, Wahunsenacah wanted to expand the Powhatan kingdom south into Eastern Chesapeake territory.

He also knew that war with the English was coming...a war that would end up lasting for five long, bloody years.

If Smith found the surviving lost colonists living happily among the Chesapeake people, it would give Wahunsenacah's enemies a good reason to join forces...an alliance of Algonquian and English foes whose combined strength might overwhelm Wahunsenacah's forces.

When Smith made clear his intention to find the lost colonists, Wahunsenacah knew he had to act quickly.

He dispatched as many as **four hundred soldiers** to sweep through Chowanoke territory, with a single purpose:

Find the lost colonists living among the Natives, and **wipe them out.**

Native stories from decades later recount a terrible swath of destruction as Powhatan warriors slaughtered more than two hundred Tuscaroras and nearly wiped out the Chesapeakes—stories that may stem from this event.

Was that the war party sent by Wahunsenacah to eliminate the lost colonists?

A Powhatan who traveled to England in early 1609...

...the same time that Smith sent his two deputies on their last search...

...suggests that it **was.**

The Powhatan, whose name was **Machumps**, was visiting the colony secretary and filling him in on what was happening among the Algonquian people.

So a bunch of the settlers from Roanoke lived among the Indians for twenty years...

...but then Wahunsenacah **slaughtered** them all when the Jamestown folks arrived.

According to Machumps, however, seven of the lost colonists survived, protected by a powerful chief named Eyanoco, who valued their skill at working **copper**...

...four men, two boys, and one young woman.

Perhaps the descendants of these seven became part of the Tuscarora Nation, which in turn became part of other Native groups.

It's likely the colonists, as well as the enslaved people set free by Sir Francis Drake, left children among the Natives who took them in.

One report from 1612 suggests that Powhatan **spared the children** in his raids.

Even if all the **adult** colonists were wiped out, many **children** might have been born during the twenty years of peace, and **they** may have had children of their **own**.

The **Lumbee Indians** of North Carolina claim descent from these youngsters.

But the true fate of the colonists is still unproven. There is evidence and there are stories, but the only way we will ever know for sure is to **keep investigating** using all of the tools at our disposal:

records, archeology, historical study, and, most important, **imagination**.

There are **many** mysteries surrounding the Lost Colony.

What happened to the people whom Drake saved from slavery?

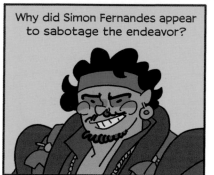

Why did Simon Fernandes appear to sabotage the endeavor?

And, the question that has baffled people for more than four hundred years...

What happened to the colonists?

What's **your** theory?

Roanoke: How do we know what we know?

An afterword from author Chris Schweizer

For four hundred years, people have been studying and writing about the people who lived in the ill-fated colony of Roanoke. These books, artworks, documents, and articles became my **sources**—the information I used to write and illustrate this graphic novel. So I wanted to elaborate on where some of this information comes from.

The first and most important sources that I used were **primary sources**.

This means that they were made during the time period I was studying. The surviving watercolors by Governor John White were very helpful, and you can see them for yourself in the book *A New World* by Kim Sloan. Sadly, many of White's drawings did not survive! Remember the contract on page 89, where the colonists promised to take care of his stuff? Well, they broke that promise; he found it buried, dug up, and strewn about the abandoned fort, ruined forever by rain and exposure to the elements.

Other primary sources include Thomas Harriot's descriptions of the Carolinas and their people and Richard Hakluyt's documentation of the venture, as well as letters and other documents pertaining

to the Roanoke Colony. These are all collected in *The Roanoke Voyages, 1584–1590*.

The next type of source is called a **secondary source**. These are writings about a subject by experts and historians who are analyzing, curating, or interpreting information that was originally found in primary sources, and through other means like archaeology. Secondary sources are a great way to learn the basics of a subject along with how it fits in the larger context of related history. If you're doing a report on Roanoke, the book you're reading right now is a secondary source!

We also rely on **archaeological evidence**. One example where archaeology helps us is regarding the very long dugout canoes. Harriot described them as being far longer (and heavier) than modern scholars believed, but in 1992 a group of archaeologists unearthed thirty canoes in Lake Phelps, North Carolina, and the canoes were just as long as (and longer than) they'd been described!

Archaeologists have unearthed many objects on Roanoke Island that give us a richer and more detailed picture of human habitation there.

Even evidence that we've had for hundreds of years can yield new findings! In 2012, while preparing John White's watercolors for a museum exhibit, experts placed White's map of the area on a lightbox to examine some patches, and underneath one of the patches discovered a drawing of a fort. Does this mean that the patch reveals the precise location of the colony? Or does it mean that the colonists decided to build it somewhere else, and White covered the old drawing because there was no fort there?

In this book, I speculated about what might've happened to Roanoke. But I also speculated on other things, too!

- We don't know what Manteo or Wanchese looked like, so I made them up, using White's watercolors of Carolina people as a starting point.

- There's no drawing, diagram, or map of the colony, so I had to make up what I thought it would look like using descriptions of the types of buildings that we know were in it, shapes used by Ralph Lane in other forts, and other historical tools.

- We don't know that Manteo and Wanchese ever met Elizabeth in person, but I thought it would be more fun if they did. We don't have any evidence that they didn't meet, after all!

Even some of the most outlandish theories have some primary sources to back them up. Here's a centuries-old woodcut showing the space battle over Germany that I mentioned on page 107!

There were more UFO sightings in Korea almost fifty years later. Since some people think aliens abducted the colonists, I thought these accounts would give that theory a little more substance.

Thank you for joining me as we attempt to unravel the mystery!

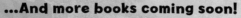